MW00462951

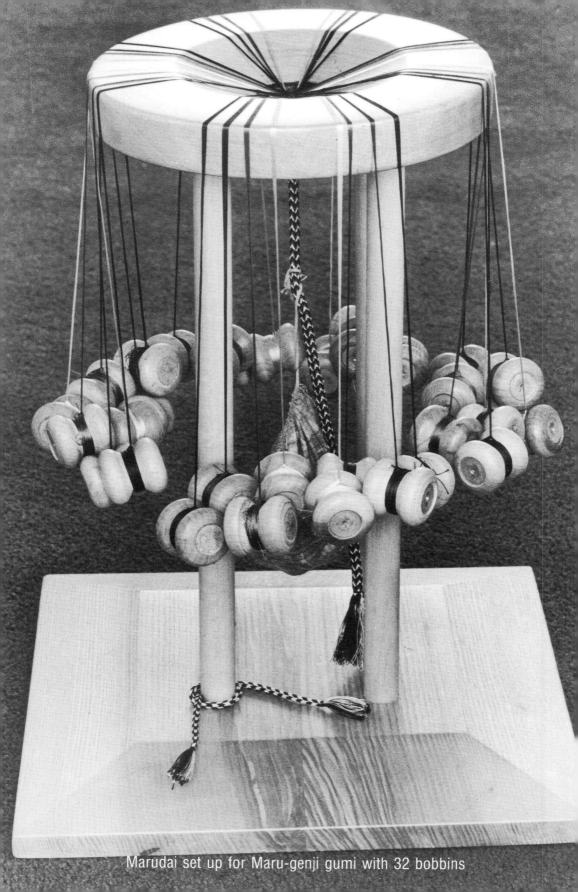

Marudai set up for Maru-genji gumi with 32 bobbins

KUMIHIMO

Japanese silk braiding techniques

Catherine Martin

BASIC MARUDAI BRAIDS

Lark Books
Asheville, North Carolina

Published in the United States in 1991 by Lark Books,
50 College Street, Asheville, NC 28801.

Copyright © Catherine Martin 1986

All rights reserved. No part of this publication may be reproduced, stored in a
retrieval system, transmitted in any form or by any means, electronic, mechanical,
photocopying, recording or otherwise without prior permission of the author.

ISBN 0-937274-59-3

To. O.G.B.

Calligraphy by Kyoko Akatsu Read

Black and white photography by Setsuo Kato
Color photography by David Cripps

All braids photographed were dyed with natural dyes and braided by Catherine
Martin.

Dyes used: Madder
               Lac
               Cochineal
               Golden Rod
               Walnut
               Shibuki
               Zakuro
               Fushi
               Tangara
               Logwood
               Indigo (Japanese)
               Indigo (Indian)

Front and Back Cover: A selection of braids made on a marudai.

Printed in Hong Kong by Oceanic Graphic Printing

CONTENTS

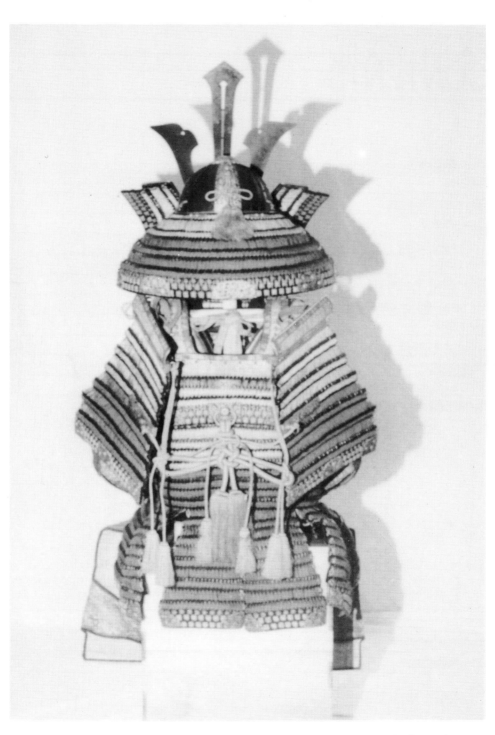

Traditional Japanese armour reproduced by kind permission of
John Anderson.

INTRODUCTION

In recent years there has been a steady flow of information about many aspects of Japanese culture conveyed to those outside Japan through television documentaries, fictional series, films, exhibitions and books; to the extent where many would, for example, recognise a suit of samurai armour as being Japanese. Very few of those, however, would also realise the astonishing fact that traditional armour is literally held together with a series of hand-made silk braids, all created to fulfil the basic principles of Japanese crafts, that of combining function with beauty.

Kumihimo encompasses many techniques of braid-making on four different looms which are still surprisingly little known or understood outside Japan, and yet these techniques have provided the world with some of its most complex and elegant silk braids, with tremendous possibilities for use with textiles. It is a difficult word to translate satisfactorily, being a compound made up of two Chinese characters. The first, *kumi*, literally means 'coming together' and the second, *himo*, on its own describes any length of string, cord, rope or braid. Together they form an independent proper noun which strictly refers to one particular way of making braids, that of 'oblique interlacing'. Cords made using other methods all have specific names, such as *yorihimo* (twisted), *amihimo* (knitted), *orihimo* (woven) and *kukehimo* (whipped), but only experts are familiar with them, and in Japan, kumihimo is the name in general use for Japanese braiding.

Although a study of kumihimo will obviously be of interest to those already working in weaving and related textile crafts, it will also appeal to those attracted to oriental philosophy and meditation, as the very nature of the craft must be thought of as a discipline in itself as well as a means to produce beautiful work. Because kumihimo has such a wide non-specialist appeal I have tried to convey the information in a clear and approachable way by avoiding the use of many of the technical terms used in either Japanese or English for various constructions and processes, but retaining the essence of the poetry and refinement so redolent of kumihimo. Comprehensive instructions are given covering all aspects of preparation, making and finishing for 12 braids including round, square and flat ones, which can be made using up to 16 bobbins on a *marudai*, the round-topped loom which is the simplest and most versatile of all the Japanese braiding devices.

Although there are many braids which can be made with 4, 8, 12 and 16 bobbins on a marudai, the selection of twelve described in detail and accompanied by diagrams has been based on those I use most often in my work when using up to 16 bobbins, and which I feel have the most potential. Twelve may not seem very many, but they all have their own characteristics, and to learn how to make them well and without mistakes will take time. Through this process, though, ideas will spring out concerning colour combinations and development of the actual braid, and for possible applications, where they can be highly effective. It is in any case far more rewarding to concentrate on producing a few, fine, even braids than to have a larger repertoire of superficially learnt, badly made braids.

My study of kumihimo took place in Japan, where I lived for four years, but it was in England where I first saw a marudai. It belonged to Lucy Goffin, and was sitting unused in her workshop. It had been a gift, and although she knew that it was a copy of a Japanese loom she knew little of the techniques involved and suggested that as I was living in Japan perhaps I could find out about Japanese braiding techniques. I am indebted to her for this suggestion, as, intrigued by the proposal, I returned to Tokyo determined to follow it up. It was through another friend, Maïtou Barrett, that I was given an introduction to the Dōmyō School and its director, Mr Issei Yamaoka, who has been responsible for analysing and reconstructing many ancient Japanese braids. Through Mr Yamaoka's generosity I was allowed to study under the personal supervision of Mrs Katsuko Dōmyō, the hereditary head of the school; an immense privilege for which I shall always be grateful. Once I had seen the incredible range of beautiful silk braids which can be made with Japanese techniques I embarked on the school's four-year course and became the first non-Japanese to graduate from the exacting training on all looms, making historical braids and dyeing with natural dyes.

On returning to England three years ago I set up my kumihimo workshop in Herefordshire where I dye and weave with Japanese equipment, adapting the traditional Japanese techniques to express my own creative ideas. During this period I have been asked to give many lectures and workshops, and have been quite overwhelmed by the widespread interest in and enthusiasm for kumihimo, not only on the part of people in Britain but also in many other countries. Realising the frustration of those wanting to learn but with no immediate access either to teachers or to accurate information, I decided to publish a manual which describes all the stages in making a braid on a marudai, the most popular of the Japanese looms, from the initial preparations to the finishing touches, for such comprehensive guidance has never been available in English before.

Nor, for that matter, is it readily available even in Japanese, for the popular kumihimo manuals on the market deal mostly with the various *kumikata* or methods of weaving, as these glossy publications with their excellent diagrams are directed towards a rapidly growing market: that of the thousands of Japanese women who are learning kumihimo in schools up and down the country where they are taught how to make *obi-shime,* which are the braids used to tie round the *obi* or stiff sash worn with a kimono; or at an advanced stage to make *haori-himo,* used to tie the front of a traditional jacket worn over kimono by both men and women. The lengths of these braids are standard, but the width depends on the type of braid. The silk used to make them is sold by the schools already dyed and usually measured, wound and divided; so the student has only to choose from the combinations of colours available and to tie and cut the silk before attaching it to the bobbins and beginning to braid.

Here the situation is different as those interested in braiding want to make their own braids in many different widths and lengths for a variety of purposes.

Therefore this manual contains advice and instructions for the decisions which have to be made before the yarn can be measured, wound, divided and cut, and then transferred to the marudai. Both the authentic Japanese ways and my own adaptations are described, with comments on the advantages and disadvantages of both.

This manual is not intended to supplant the teacher of kumihimo, and if expert help is available, especially in the early stages, it is strongly recommended. Nevertheless it contains much information which will be helpful both to those who are already learning and to those who wish to make a start on braiding.

The teaching I received at Japan's most prestigious school of braiding over a long period was invaluable. All those who guided me were invariably generous towards one they must have thought of as an impatient, persistent and demanding student and taught me many braids on all the looms including complex historical reconstructions which have yet to be described in print even in Japan. I remain in touch with them, of course, and continue to be indebted to the Dōmyō School for equipment and research materials. One way in which I can express this indebtedness is, it seems to me, to share some of the remarkable knowledge my teachers communicated to me with others outside Japan. This is therefore the first of a planned series of books on kumihimo. Although it is intended as a practical guide, I should be astonished if those who follow its suggestions and start to braid do not soon become conscious of the pleasure and the tranquillity to be derived from practising an art which is so ancient and yet so new.

Untwisted silk dyed with plants that were used in the 8th century for braids found in the Shōsō-in collection. The name of the dye is attached to each skein and the dyeing was carried out by Mr Shin-ichiro Dōmyō

HISTORY

At the entrance to each of the tens of thousands of Shinto shrines in Japan stands at least one gateway or *torii,* made of wood or stone. These gateways range in size from about that of an English church lych gate to gigantic constructions forty or fifty feet high supported on massive pillars a metre or more in girth; but one thing common to many is a heavy, simply-made rope suspended between those pillars. From the rope hang small zig-zag pieces of white paper. Together they protect the shrine precincts from invasion by evil spirits, and other, smaller versions of the same talismans are to be found here and there within those precincts, as a sign of reverence and to give added protection to certain trees and rocks regarded as sacred, as well as at the entrance to the innermost sanctuary. Ropes, plaits and knots have since ancient times played a vital role in many aspects of Japanese culture, and the incorporation of silk braiding techniques into the traditional way of life must therefore have represented a natural progression.

The earliest indications of the use of twined fibres in Japan can be seen on pots discovered at sites all over the country and dating from the initial Jōmon period (about 7,500 B.C.). Vegetable fibres were twisted and wound round the pots while still wet to provide a decorative pattern, and sometimes remained in place during firing. An alternative and more economical way of impressing a decoration was by the use of fibres wound round a bamboo stick which was rolled on to the soft surface of the unfired clay. When the Japanese began to cultivate rice they put discarded rice straw to many uses, including matting, and to this day dried fish and other foodstuffs are sold in the most high-class food stores still laced with simple elegance into the straw with which they were originally hung. The Japanese delight in the ancient practice of twisting and knotting natural fibres and putting them to both functional and decorative use has not diminished over the centuries.

The earliest surviving evidence of the incorporation of braids into Japanese costume is provided by *haniwa,* clay figures about 1.5m high which have been found in burial mounds dating from the 4th to 6th centuries A.D. Representations of warriors were found dressed in prototype samurai armour with its distinctive shape and the use of braids at various points.

One of the earliest silk braids of the Far East was found in Korea and dates from about 50 B.C., and it shows that techniques were already advanced in that country at the time. Formal silk-braiding was not however introduced into Japan until the 7th and 8th centuries, and then as with so many art forms, the techniques adopted were both Korean and Chinese. Preoccupied as the early Japanese were with knotting and tying, braid-making must have appealed to them tremendously, and a distinctively Japanese tradition of kumihimo was soon established. The earliest surviving Japanese braids constitute an important part of the great *Shōsō-in* collection of priceless art objects of the Nara period (710-794). Although the silk has of course deteriorated, analysis of dyes and techniques has enabled reconstructions to be made. These demonstrate a range of different types and shapes of braid and their probable uses, since some of the originals were attached to specific objects, which included those found on garments used by priests, musicians and dancers, and many used for hanging various items like pendants, cords for tying bags, and tassels on religious banners. Most were made on a marudai using strong colours, with olives, oranges, browns and purples predominating.

During the Heian period (794-1185) and in the early part of the Kamakura period (1185-1333) artistic and social structures became less derivative and foreign influences were less popular. One of the most distinguished braids, the diamond-patterned *Kara kumi* was one of the first braids that was uniquely Japanese, and those that followed became highly complex. Lying undiscovered in temples, shrines and tombs until this century, they represent the highest flowering of Japanese braiding. No descriptions of the *kumikata* or methods of braiding survived, and so they had to be painstakingly re-created by the Dōmyō family, using between 42-80 bobbins for each of the following, which are named after the temple or shrine in which they were found: *Chuzon-ji gumi, Shitenno-ji gumi, Saidai-ji gumi, Itsukushima gumi* and *Chion-in gumi.* These are all exquisitely beautiful braids and considering when they were devised, exhibit remarkably sophisticated techniques.

The Japanese aesthetic ideal of combining function and beauty is clearly displayed in the many different methods of braiding used for traditional armour. Flat, plain braid is used to lace the components together in often elaborate colour schemes, while others are incorporated for support, linkages and fastenings. Many museums outside Japan possess at least one suit of samurai armour, and it should not therefore be difficult for most people to track one down and examine the braids at close quarters. Swords also had their specially designed braids: a flat, slightly ridged braid without a pattern was wound tightly round the hilt to provide a sure grip for these terrifyingly sharp blades, and a strong, thick, decorative braid was used to attach the scabbard to its owner's armour.

Every development in Japanese social history was reflected in the need for braids of different shapes, textures and patterns. The Edo period (1600-1868) was one of general peace and tranquillity during which the indigenous Japanese arts flourished. The traditional theatrical forms of Noh, Kabuki and Bunraku all called for sumptuous silk costumes and appropriately gorgeous braids for decoration, fastenings and for decorative knots with tassels. During this time the two-level *takadai* was invented, enabling flat, double-cloth, non-repeat patterned braids to be made for the first time. Intricate, slow to make and often with a motif worked into them, these braids had an entirely different appearance from those which had gone before. Until this time most braids had been constructed on a *marudai, kakudai* or a simple version of the *takadai*. The new braids were so complex that it is presumed that the kumihimo makers of the period specialised in certain braids. (This is still largely the case today, in that although most makers are familiar with and can make braids on any loom they tend to specialise on either the marudai or the takadai.) Edo period braids can be seen in many museums on such articles as *inrō* (tiny lacquered medicine containers) on dolls, screens, armour, swords and as ties for lacquer boxes. Quite often braids were embroidered on kimono, indicating their uses, such as ties for baskets in which insects were kept.

After 1868 the samurai class was abolished and their armour and swords sadly often relegated to junk-shops as western influences and rapid industrialisation transformed Japan. New synthetic dyes were developed and machines were devised to do all manner of things including braiding, which must have seemed as sacrilegious as it was undoubtedly economically disastrous to the traditional braid-makers. Nevertheless, with characteristic ingenuity they set about adapting many of the ancient methods in order to exploit a new market which opened up following the fashion for and virtually universal adoption by Japanese women of a very wide obi to wear with their kimono. The new obi had to be secured with a cord, and so the now ubiquitous obi-shime was devised. Short pairs of braids had been introduced as fastenings for haori jackets some time earlier, and haori braids and obi-shime together now account for most silk braids sold, although 95% of those are now machine-made. Nevertheless, there is a market for hand-made obi-shime, which are much more comfortable to wear than the machine-made variety, as the weaving naturally incorporates a stretchy element. The craft also survives through the many schools which have been opened throughout Japan in the last 12 years.

Other types of braid for special purposes are of course still being made and may be seen often in traditional contexts like the classical Japanese drama, on reconstructions of historical costumes in festivals, attached to Tea ceremony utensils and articles and garments used in religious rites, and in Sumo wrestling, where appropriately huge braids and tassels are placed at the four corners of the canopy over the ring. Decorative knots too still feature prominently in Japanese wrapping and packaging, including the beautiful envelopes used on solemn or auspicious occasions.

So the tradition lives on in Japan, with more knowing the secrets of kumihimo workshops than ever before, although the creative impulse seems to be stagnating. Outside Japan I am sure that the techniques of braiding will quickly spread and be absorbed into the western tradition of needlework, embroidery and all the other textile crafts. This should produce some interesting results and ensure a continuation of the Japanese tradition. We shall see.

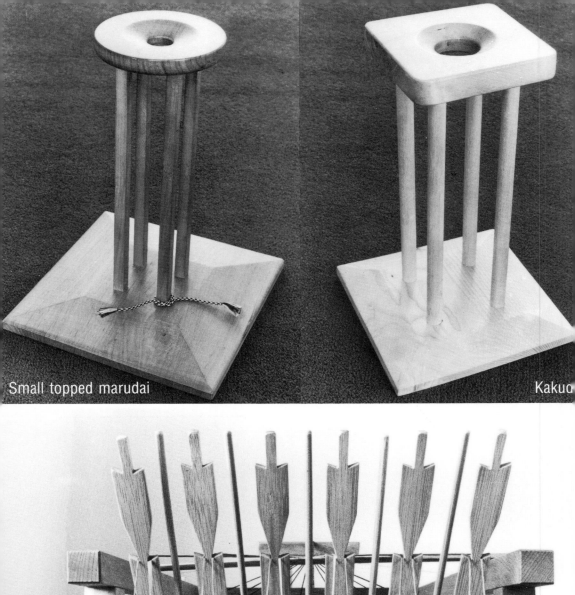

Small topped marudai   Kakuo

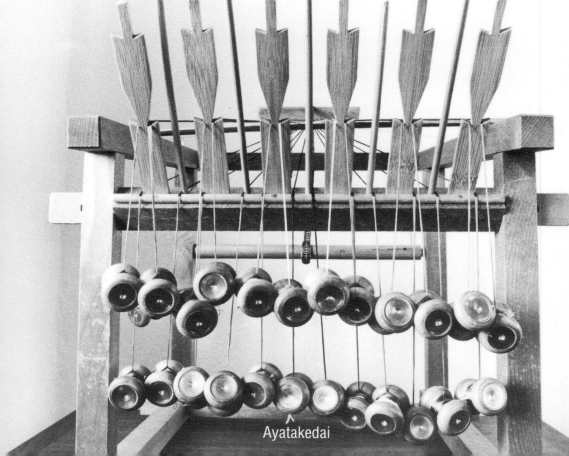

Ayatakedai

JAPANESE LOOMS

Four different types of loom are used for making braids in Japan today. Most students begin with either the marudai or the kakudai and proceed to the takadai and the ayatakedai. Here is a description of the principles of braiding and a note about each loom.

All looms are set up with a silk warp which consists of divided groups of equal numbers of strands of silk, each attached to an evenly weighted wood and lead bobbin. These are moved in certain ways to produce a type of braid. The marudai and kakudai need counterweights, but with the ayatakedai and the takadai the braid is beaten into place.

> The method of braiding defines the shape of the braid and consists of a series of movements, described as the 'sequence of braiding'.

> Different patterns can be created by using the same method but varying the arrangement of the colours used before making the first movement prescribed in the sequence of braiding.

Marudai

On this round-topped loom (*maru* = round, *dai* = stand) the weight of the bobbins is countered by a bag containing a quantity of lead weights calculated on the basis of the total weight of the bobbins. A braid is made by lifting and repositioning pairs of bobbins according to the sequence of braiding which is repeated until the required length is completed. The layout of the method of braiding indicates the number of bobbins in any one group and the position of the groups in relation to one another around the surface of the marudai. With different methods of braiding, flat, round or square braids can be made. It is possible to weave with the weight pulling the braid down below the surface of the marudai (downward braiding) or with it suspended above the surface from a pole hanging from the ceiling, in which case it is called upward braiding. All the braids described in this manual are downward braids.

Kakudai

This is a square-topped stand (*kaku* = square) which although it can be used for downward braiding is more often used for upward braiding, producing a variety of round braids counterweighted above the stand. Pairs of bobbins are moved together.

Ayatakedai

Aya means design and *take* bamboo, and this 'bamboo design' stand is so called because the bobbins are hung from six separated pieces of notched and carved bamboo attached to a square wooden frame and facing the kneeling braid-maker. Each row of weaving is produced by moving the bobbins in pairs from one notch to another and the row of stitches is 'fixed' by passing and crossing two thin weft strands attached to heavy bobbins inside the braid. A *hera* (a long, flat piece of bamboo) is used to beat the braid into place. Braids made on an ayatakedai are flat, strong and often plain or with a textured finish.

Takadai

Taka means high, and this loom is the only braiding device at which the weaver can sit rather than operate from a kneeling position, though kneeling was so instinctive for Japanese that the traditional takadai still incorporates a platform to make this possible. On each side of the braid-maker are two rows (one higher than the other) of moveable blocks of wood with pegs set into them to divide the strands of yarn. The bobbins are passed singly from one side to the other through a hand-created passage or shed and the braid is then beaten into place with a hera. No counterweight is required, and braids can be made using either one level on each side or both. Only flat braids can be made on this loom. Strong flat braids are produced using one level, and these were used for lacing on armour. By using both a double-cloth braid can be made, often with a motif pattern repeated at will rather than appearing regularly as with the other looms.

Takadai

EQUIPMENT

Most Japanese homes are much smaller than those in the west, and living and sleeping on the floor in the traditional way means that many objects can and must be packed away when not in use. Bedding is stored in cupboards during the day, flat floor-cushions are stacked one upon another until needed, and even the legs of low Japanese tables can often be folded flat to provide more space in a room when the table is propped on its side against the wall. This economy in the use of space applies to many Japanese activities and the principle dictates the construction of the equipment for kumihimo. Looms can be taken apart and stored when not in use, *kowaku* (the square yarn holders) can be hung, and so on. One of the advantages of learning kumihimo as distinct from other forms of weaving, particularly on a marudai, is that an extensive array of braids can be made with very little equipment, while the marudai itself may easily be carried from one place to another.

All that is needed in order to make the braids described in this book is a marudai, bobbins, a chopstick, weights, yarn and a few miscellaneous items to be found in most homes. Detailed descriptions of the necessary equipment follow.

The Marudai

The marudai is a wooden braiding device consisting of a smooth round surface shelving at a certain point to a central aperture and supported by four pillars fastened securely in a sturdy base. Japanese marudai are made from cherry or maple, and any substitute must be a light close-grained wood if the top is to be smooth enough. The wood from a sycamore tree makes excellent marudai tops.

The dimensions of a standard marudai are:

> Height: 40cm
> Diameter of top: 20.5cm   Diameter of aperture: 3cm
> Flat surface at top: 5cm, shelving to 1cm at central aperture
> Thickness of top: 2.5cm at outer edge
> Size of base: 30cm square
> Thickness of base: 2cm at centre, 1.5cm on outside edge
> Diameter of pillars: 2cm (outside distance on base 11cm)

The usual height for a Japanese-made marudai is about 45cm, but as most non-Japanese find sitting on the floor more comfortable than the traditional kneeling position, a height of 40cm usually suits the average westerner better. The diameter of the top depends entirely on the number of bobbins being used and their size: the standard top accommodates up to 32 x 70gm bobbins easily, but I use three different marudai, with tops of 15cm, 20.5cm and 30cm in diameter respectively. The base of a marudai needs to be solid as the total weight of the bobbins used can be considerable. A marudai is not difficult to make, but the utmost care must be taken with the finishing. Not only the top and the central aperture but also the base must be well sanded and smooth, or they will surely damage or snag any silk coming into contact with them. A word to the sceptical: although it is of course technically possible to stand or to sit on a chair while using a marudai (of a different and appropriate height), I am not convinced that this position can ever result in good work. Evenness in braiding seems to flow from a low centre of gravity such as that provided by kneeling or sitting on a cushion on the floor.

Bobbins

Japanese bobbins are made of wood able to withstand high temperatures and weighted with lead that is cast into them. A cross-section shows that the lead is cast in the shape of a dumb-bell so that the bobbin will hang evenly from the loom. Bobbins are made in various sizes and weights to suit various looms and the weight dictates the number of fine strands of silk to be attached to them. Good bobbins are essential for any braiding, and the best available in Japan are those made for the Dōmyō School which needs a greater range of sizes than the other schools to meet the special requirements for reconstructing ancient braids. All their bobbins are smaller and neater than those of other schools which I have examined. They are made to high standards of consistency within a weight tolerance of 1gm. It is not difficult to imagine the unnevenness which results in a braid made with bobbins of different weights, and though with careful calculation and in expert hands interesting effects can be obtained by using them deliberately, evenly weighted bobbins are essential for beginners and for all normal braiding. The 70gm size is generally used on a marudai and is also suitable for the other three kumihimo looms. When working in silk, the relation of the weight of bobbin to the number of strands used is as follows:

37gm:	3- 8 strands of fine silk per bobbin
70gm:	9-18 strands of fine silk per bobbin
100gm:	18-30 strands of fine silk per bobbin

It is not a good idea to try to make tiny braids with 70gm bobbins: the weight is far too great for the silk and a good result will not be obtained. 37gm bobbins or lighter plain wooden ones are recommended.

The bobbins made in this country which I have so far seen are certainly not suitable for fine silk braiding and are a poor substitute for the authentic Japanese version, which, though expensive, do not deteriorate with age: quite the reverse, for the more they are used and handled the smoother they become. Before using new bobbins a cotton leader thread must be wound round each bobbin and the silk attached to this. This is to make it possible for all the silk to be used up while still allowing the bobbins to hang at the appropriate working height from the marudai surface. Medium weight crochet thread is ideal for this purpose, a double 40cm length being wound around the bobbin as illustrated.

Weights

To provide the central counterweight which must be attached to the braid throughout its construction, lead weights are placed inside a small bag secured with a drawstring ending in a large knot. When starting a braid the bag is attached to the end of the silk by a picture or S-shaped hook. As the braid grows this is taken off and the bag tied around the growing braid. The size of the bag does to some extent depend on the number of weights to be used, but the size illustrated is suitable when making the braids in this book using up to 32 bobbins of 37gm or 70gm.

pattern

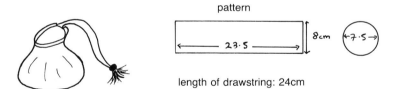

length of drawstring: 24cm

The bag should be made of fairly tough cotton or silk and sewn securely, particularly at the opening for the drawstring, as it has to cope with some strain. For the drawstring a length of hand-made 8-bobbin braid is the best (I use the method of braiding known as *mitake gumi*) but any fairly fine braid can be used. Bear in mind that the smoother it is, the more difficult it will be to tie it around the braid being made without having it slip off and end up with a resounding thud on the base of the marudai.

The weight of the filled bag should in general be just under half the total weight of the bobbins being used, but it is difficult to be specific about this as different braid-makers' individual actions can vary considerably, with some producing much tighter, stiffer braids than others using identical equipment. Ideally, the place at which the strands cross over each other, known as the **point of braiding** should be just below the upper edge of the central aperture in the marudai, but it is advisable to adjust weights when making samples so as to be able to achieve the appropriate degree of stiffness for a braid's intended purpose. Once embarked on a complete braid, however, **never** change the counterweight as even a small adjustment will affect both appearance and flexibility.

> The heavier the counterweight, the looser the tension of the weaving will be.

> The lighter the counterweight, the tighter the tension of the weaving will be.

In Japan special lead discs are used, but the lead weights available in many shapes and sizes at any fishing tackle shop are perfectly satisfactory though you may need to convert ounces into grams (since the weight of the bobbins is measured in grams). A number of the same weight (the round balls are most useful), plus a few smaller ones, will provide greater versatility in use. Mark the weight on each so as to be able to keep accurate records.

Miscellaneous items

While working I always sit or kneel on a cushion and have a tray beside me containing the following:

1 A reel of fairly fine crochet cotton, for dividing and tying the strands of silk when preparing the yarn for the marudai, and for tying off at the end of a braid. The cotton must be strong, or it will break when you are tying the silk firmly. Ordinary sewing cotton will not do.

2 Small sharp embroidery scissors

3 A chopstick, which is an essential item in the Japanese way of braiding. It should be smooth and preferably lacquered or made of plastic. Chinese chopsticks can be used but tend to be on the large side, and a wooden knitting needle might make a better substitute.

4 A picture hook or other small s-shaped hook, for attaching the counterweight to the silk before beginning to braid.

5 A notebook for writing notes during all stages of braid-making, so that a record is kept of the method and colours used, bobbins, weights, length of yarn cut, experiments and the effect of changing the position of colours on the marudai before starting a braid. To supplement this a few coloured pencils, an eraser and a coin to trace a circle to represent the top of the marudai or a stencil with circles of various sizes bought from any good stationer are useful.

6 A tape measure.

7 A piece of braid or ribbon to tie around one pillar of the marudai, indicating the side of the marudai facing you when starting to braid.

YARN AND DYES

Kumihimo has always been thought of as one of the most refined and elegant of the Japanese crafts, and although cotton and linen yarns have been used in the past for certain specific purposes, the majority of braids have always been made of silk. From the examples preserved since the 8th century in the Shōsō-in Imperial treasure house in the city of Nara we know that unspun silk or thicker hand-twisted silk was used for early braids, the former producing soft, flexible braids but with patterns less clearly defined than those achieved with the twisted silk. Nowadays a fine, reeled, 3-ply, highly-twisted silk is used for hand-braiding and is sold in many colours through the kumihimo schools, some of which also sell undyed silk in 25gm skeins to those who wish to dye their own, though this is impracticable for the majority of students who live in small houses or flats in urban areas.

While learning how to make reconstructions of the ancient braids of Japan I became increasingly dissatisfied when using synthetically dyed silk, feeling that naturally dyed yarn would be more sympathetic to the work. After all, natural dyes were the only way of producing colour in textiles until the mid-nineteenth century, by which time most of the really beautiful Japanese braids had been devised; and in any case the quality of natural colours seems to me to be far more beautiful than the sharpness of modern dyes.

Kusakizome or natural dyeing has always been part of the traditional way of life in Japan, and interestingly enough, recent years have seen a resurgence of interest in it with the growing awareness of the extent to which some of the most treasured traditional crafts have been eroded by modern technology. I studied Japanese kusakizome methods in both Kyoto and with Mr Shin-ichiro Dōmyō in Tokyo, and became fascinated by the unpredictability of it all; the surprising colours emerging from murky pots, the never-ending experiments to try to achieve subtle but glowing colours, and the difference in tones yielded by the same plants from year to year depending on the weather. To realise that it is impossible ever to obtain the same colour twice is something to be enjoyed rather than to despair over (unless produced for a commercial enterprise where exact colour matching is necessary), particularly with kumihimo where the more colours that are available, the more interesting combinations can be woven. As only small amounts of silk are used for braids compared with other forms of hand-weaving or knitting, the vast quantities of natural dyestuffs so often described in dye recipes are fortunately not required, and only a small dyeing area, with jugs and bowls rather than huge tubs and buckets is sufficient to work in.

The silk I dye comes from the mountains of Kanagawa Prefecture to the west of Tokyo, from a family which has been involved in silk production for generations, and nothing like it is available in Europe at present. It is expensive but of an excellent quality, and is supplied in 25gm skeins. I usually wind it into smaller quantities of 5 or 10 grams for test dyeing before using a larger amount for colours which predominate in my work.

After dyeing, when the silk is completely dry, it is wound on to *kowaku* which are free-standing square wooden yarn holders, 15cm high. Two medieval-looking devices, a *tombo* and a *zaguri* made from wood and bamboo are needed for this process. Then the measuring, winding and dividing process known as **warping** can be carried out.

Dyeing and winding are time-consuming processes not to be recommended except to those who want to learn everything about kumihimo. For the majority of my students who want to make silk braids to complement their own work and for my own samples I use the same quality of silk ready-dyed and wound on to convenient reels like large cotton reels. This is available from Japan in 220 superb colours. As noted earlier, the ready-warped silk used by Japanese kumihimo students is available only in predetermined, inconvenient lengths.

Other yarns may of course be used for making braids using Japanese techniques and can, in the right hands, be most effective. Nevertheless, most of the braiding I have seen utilising other – and particularly synthetic – yarns seems crude in comparison with the beautiful silk braids I learned to make and saw so often in Japan. There is one crucial and objective difference: proper kumihimo yarn is shiny, incredibly smooth and flexible, which means that clear vibrant patterns are produced by the braiding. Any slightly rough or hairy yarn will produce hairy braids with a muddier appearance, obscuring the clean pattern of the braid, but this may be the desired result.

Throughout this book I refer to silk, both because my experience is based on using it and because I feel it is the only fibre for true Japanese kumihimo. However, everybody creating braids must use whatever yarns seem appropriate to their work, which is exactly what I am doing when I use silk. The equipment and method of preparation will be largely the same, though thicker yarns may call for larger, heavier bobbins and counterweights, with the necessary adjustments being calculated. Thicker yarn will of course be much quicker to work with, but the principles of braiding remain the same.

Kowaku

WARPING

Before making a braid, certain decisions about its finished dimensions and colours must be taken. Then the silk has to be measured, divided into groups of usually equal numbers of strands for each bobbin, tied, and cut in such a way that it can be neatly transferred to the loom. This is the warping process. Then, the groups can be separated out, and each one tied with a special knot to a cotton thread wound round the bobbin. When all the bobbins have been tied to the silk they can be wound up and hung from the loom, arranged in groups of colours for the chosen pattern and method of braiding. The process is the same for all the looms used in Japanese braiding.

Choices

A wide variety of shapes, sizes, textures and patterns are available to the braid-maker, and choices concerning the required length, thickness, colour content and the number of bobbins to be used always have to be made before any practical steps can be taken for the preparation of the yarn for the loom. This can be quite complex and it is discussed fully in a later chapter, as it will seem far more relevant after some practical experience of making a braid. Bearing this in mind suggestions concerning dimensions and patterns are given for making samples of braids described, with the intention of simplifying the first attempt at making each of the braids.

Before warping can take place the following must be decided:

1   Length of yarn to be cut

2   Number of bobbins to be used

3   Number of strands to be used for each bobbin

4   Number of colours

5   Number of bobbins for each colour

Once the details have been written down, warping can begin.

Japanese Warping Equipment

The Japanese use a pair of *bodai* for measuring and dividing the silk. These are two identical smooth wooden poles set into heavy, weighted square bases and with removable steel attachments which slot into the top of each pole. These are extremely useful at many stages in kumihimo. The bodai can be placed at any distance apart and will not move while the silk is being wound around them. Since this is their main function, it will be obvious that heavy clamps on a table or moveable pegs on a board if rigid enough will serve as substitutes. Bodai are depicted in the illustrations for the warping section and their measurements are as follows:

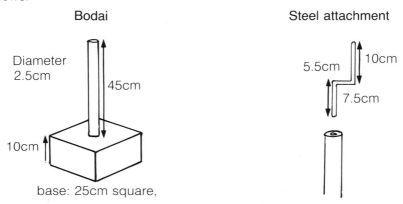

Bodai — Diameter 2.5cm, 45cm, 10cm, base: 25cm square,

Steel attachment — 5.5cm, 10cm, 7.5cm

The traditional way of warping in Japan always takes place from a kneeling position with the kowaku on the floor. The strand of fine silk is then unwound and taken up and over a horizontal pole hanging from the ceiling and brought down to wind around the bodai. This ensures a free flowing supply of yarn, but as most of those following these warping instructions will be holding reels of silk or other yarn in their hands, I have adapted the method accordingly. If cones or reels are free-standing, then the method of winding over a pole is to be recommended. My pole is a carefully sanded broomstick, suspended by equal lengths of braid at each end, knotted and looped on to two hooks in the ceiling. The pole should be level (otherwise the yarn will inevitably move to the lowest part and might become entangled in the hanging braid) and just above head height.

In my work I use three related but different methods of warping, depending basically on the length of the silk to be warped, and all three methods are described here. I would direct those making braids for the first time to the first method and to ignore the others until a later stage because of potential problems, especially if using fine slippery silk. Although not a particularly tidy or organised person by nature, I have learned the hard way that unless the stages of instructions are followed implicitly and everything is put away after it has been used, certain problems will occur and put the braid-maker into a somewhat cross frame of mind, which is not a good state to be in when preparing for kumihimo.

Method 1

This is an adaptation of the Japanese way of warping which I developed after several disasters when first learning the authentic way. The silk is prepared for the marudai with a loop at one end, and this ensures safety at the next stage when attaching and winding up the bobbins. The only disadvantage of this method is that the maximum length of silk which can comfortably be measured from a kneeling or sitting position is about 1.50 metres. For warping more than this length I use the Japanese way; but since most of those learning how to braid will in any case wish to make shorter lengths for experiments with colour, patterns and sizes it is advisable to try this method before using the others.

The principle is to wind the yarn in a **clockwise** direction round the two poles of the bodai (or substitute) the number of times needed for the number of strands per bobbin, bearing in mind that **each** winding provides the yarn for **two** bobbins, one on either side of the poles. Cotton thread is tied around the yarn to divide the groups off. After repeating the winding a certain number of times (depending on the number of bobbins to be used for the braid) and dividing the groups each time, all the silk is tied together at one end forming a loop which becomes the beginning tassel to the braid and the yarn is cut at the other.

A word of warning: warping for the first time seems complicated. So, go slowly and follow the instructions and diagrams carefully if there is nobody to help you, and make sure that you count accurately for each winding. After the warping and putting on the bobbins has been completed, the whole process will seem much clearer and more logical the next time round.

Here is the process in detail for making a 16-bobbin braid such as *Maru-genji gumi* in two colours using black silk for 8 bobbins and red for the other 8. The length to be cut is 1 metre and there are to be 12 strands of silk per bobbin.

The equipment needed is: yarn, 2 bodai plus steel attachment or substitutes, a tape measure, notebook and pencil, a reel of crochet cotton, scissors and a chopstick.

1   Write down the following:

> Method of braiding: Maru-genji gumi
> No of bobbins: 16
> No of strands per bobbin: 12
>
> Black: 1+2, 3+4, 5+6, 7+8
> Red: 1+2, 3+4, 5+6, 7+8

2　Set the poles of the bodai 1 metre apart.

3　Cut 5 lengths each of about 25cm of cotton thread and place them at the right-hand side of the warping equipment.

4　Picking up the reel of black silk in the right hand, hold the end of the silk with the left hand against the outside of the LH pole about two-thirds of the way up, and **keep it there** throughout initial winding.

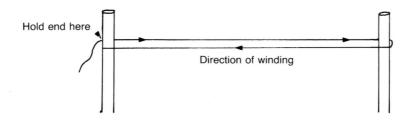

Hold end here

Direction of winding

By holding the top of the reel firmly, allow the silk to unwind itself through your fingers as the reel is carried in a clockwise direction around the poles, making sure that each time it is wound it secures the cut end on the LH side. Keep count as the silk is wound. This process of winding will seem awkward at first, but you will soon discover how to establish a smooth winding rhythm. After about 5 windings the cut end will be kept in place by the wound silk. During this process the silk must be kept taut but not stretched in any way. After the 12th round, slip the reel of silk through the centre of the wound yarn at the left-hand side, where the thread will be kept in place by the winding. Place the reel on the base of the bodai. The silk should now be wound neatly and the strands should be close together at the poles.

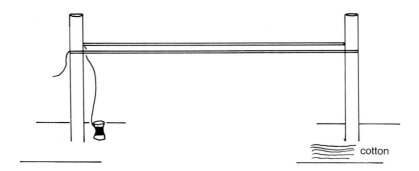

cotton

While winding with the right hand, the left hand can be used to gently push down the newly wound silk so that subsequent windings are close together.

5   In order to separate the wound silk from the next winding, take one of the lengths of cotton, double it and place it on top of the wound strands facing you about 25cm from the RH pole.

6   Pull the cut ends through the loop and pull. Repeat for the other side of the yarn, with the second piece of cotton. This method of fastening, known as a half-hitch or lark's head, is used for many different purposes in kumihimo. When tying groups of silk tightly together use this method over itself many times for a firm tie.

7   Cross off 'Black 1+2' in the notebook.

8   Carefully retrieve the reel of black silk from its resting position up through the middle of the wound silk and continue winding round the poles another 12 times, counting accurately, and replace the silk in its resting position again.

9   To separate off the new groups of silk, pull the cotton thread down so that the group previously tied is completely separated from the newly wound threads and slip the ends of the cotton over the new group, pulling it through towards you in **between** the two groups. Do make sure that **all** the strands belonging to a group of 12 are together inside the cotton dividing thread.

10 Cross off 'Black 3+4' in the book and repeat the same procedure of winding and dividing off twice more, so that the black silk has been warped for all 8 bobbins, then with the same cotton thread tie the four groups of silk together once to make one bunch with a half-hitch.

11 Leaving the reel of black silk in its resting position, repeat stages 4-10 above with the red silk, winding in a position just above the wound black silk. It will then look like this; with two identical groups of threads each side of the two poles, although the first groups to be wound will always be slacker than the last: this is inevitable.

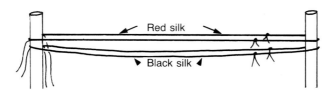

12 If you do have the attachment mentioned earlier, place it in the top of the RH pole and move the silk up on to it. Move the RH bodai away until the silk is taut again and tie all the silk together firmly with the last piece of cotton thread in a series of half-hitches, just a little way from the attachment (a).

(a)

If you do not have the attachment, tie all the silk together with the cotton, again in a series of half-hitches at the RH end of your substitute for bodai, bearing in mind that the size of the loop you are making represents the length of the tassel at the beginning of your braid (b).

(b)
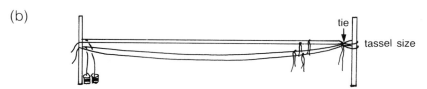

If a long tassel (more than 2cm) is required, tie two knots 1cm apart as an opening for the chopstick as illustrated (c).

(c)
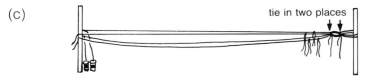

13 Taking a pair of scissors, slip the silk off the LH pole with the left hand and hold it while cutting through the centre, making sure that the ends still attached to the two reels of silk are also cut afterwards (lay the silk down and trim the cut ends if they are not all the same length).

14 Take the silk off the RH pole and insert the chopstick in the loop. It should look like this:

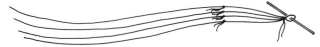

Now the silk is ready to put on the marudai, so turn to the section on **attaching the bobbins.** If it is not to be used immediately, lay it carefully aside with its chopstick in a polythene bag or hang it where it cannot be disturbed. The process as described above sounds lengthy and complex, but after a few times it becomes quite automatic. I am often asked how long it takes to prepare silk for a 16-bobbin braid with 12 strands per bobbin: the answer is about 10 minutes. If different colours are required for single bobbins, wind half the number of strands needed, separate off with cotton in the usual way, remembering to join the two halves together when attaching the groups of silk strands to the bobbins.

Method 2 – The Japanese Way

In Japan this method is used for preparing silk for any loom if more than 60cm is required, though it is more usual to be preparing the 2.70m needed to make obishime. It is also suitable for warping **odd** numbers of bobbins for certain colours if method 1 is used for the majority of the warping.

The principle differs from that of the first method in that each winding represents the length of silk for **one** bobbin only, so the division and tying of the silk takes place near the LH pole where the silk will be cut. After the silk is wound and divided it is tied **very tightly** in two places to provide an opening for the chopstick. Unless these knots are very firm, the fine silk will slip through if any pressure is put upon it while attaching it to and winding the bobbins. It was this problem which prompted me to find another way of preparing the silk, for it is no fun to try to tie back loose single strands of silk which results in an untidy start to the braid; and the first method of warping as described above does prevent potential disaster.

Assuming that you have already tried the first method, it is necessary only to note the practical differences between that and the second.

1   Use a longer end of silk placed against the LH pole than in Method No 1. After winding and dividing (which should take place about 20cm from the LH pole on the side facing you **only**), remembering that each winding represents the silk for **one** bobbin, two knots should be made in the position indicated below, about 1.5cm apart.

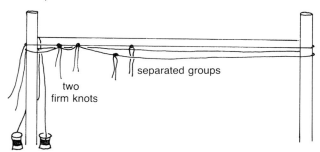

separated groups

two
firm knots

2   The silk is then cut about 3cm (depending on the length of tassel required) from the LH pole, at the point where the first end of the silk was placed before winding began.

3   If fine silk is used this long length will tangle easily, so care must be taken when transferring it to the marudai.

The longer the silk, the more difficult it is to separate out groups from one another before attaching the bobbins. So, take great care in sorting out any tangles **and do not pull the silk** otherwise it will slip through the knots made at the end of warping.

Method 3

This method is part of that used by the Japanese when preparing silk for the complicated task of making *haori-himo,* the two 16cm-long braids with 2.5cm tassels found on haori jackets, which ingeniously incorporate a loop into the braid at one end. The method is useful for preparing short lengths of silk for samples, or when making simple braids of one or two colours only. One bodai only is used (and if the steel attachment is available, insert it in the bodai and wind round it), with a finger as substitute for the other bodai. It is a fast method of warping but it is difficult to divide the silk into groups with only one free hand so if they are not divided, which does take skill, then counting has to be accurate. It is based on Method 1 (each winding of the silk representing that for **two** bobbins) and a loop is tied at one end.

Here is a description of the process.

1 Before starting to wind, have a tape measure and the lengths of cotton thread ready, and a pair of scissors nearby.

2 Holding the end of the silk in the left hand, the reel of silk is wound with the right hand around the pole and brought back to one finger of the left hand, adjusting the distance to that required for the cut length of silk for the braid.

3 When this has been established, the winding continues until the right number of strands for all the bobbins of a particular colour is reached. (For example, if 4 bobbins are to be wound with 5 strands per bobbin, then the silk needs to be wound 10 times round the pole).

4 Tie off the silk each side with cotton threads with the right hand only, keeping the left holding the silk. Place the reel of silk on the floor. Continue with the next colour warping in the same way around the pole and one finger of the left hand. When all the colours have been wound, hold the silk at the pole in one hand (letting the other end of the silk drop down), and picking up the scissors, cut the loops with the other hand. Then tie the silk all together at the pole (or attachment) as both hands are now free, and slip the resulting loop off the bodai and insert the chopstick.

The disadvantage of this method is that if dividing is too difficult to manage while winding each individual strand has to be counted before being put on the bobbins. This is a time-consuming process limiting the suitability of the method to short lengths of yarn, as long lengths of yarn tangle so easily when trying to divide them.

Attaching the bobbins

Once the silk has been warped, a space has to be cleared for the next stage: that of putting the silk on the marudai and attaching the bobbins. The equipment needed is: a marudai: 16 bobbins: the warped silk: a bag containing the counterweight: and a picture hook. The required number of bobbins should be placed away from the marudai at a distance representing the length of the cut silk. They should be set down to one side so that when the silk is brought to them they will be in a convenient place. Place a heavy weight (the counterweight in the bag is suitable) and the picture hook beside the marudai.

If the first method of warping has been used and the silk divided and counted accurately there should be no problem in separating the 4 groups and their subdivisions, attaching the bobbins to the silk and winding them up. The ends of each subdivided group of silk are tied to the cotton leader thread of the bobbin with a special knot, after which the bobbin is wound and hung from the marudai. Here is the process step by step; continuing with the example of *maru-genji gumi,* using 16 bobbins and two colours.

1   Holding the chopstick in the right hand, with a thumb on the silk so that it does not slip off, insert one end of the chopstick into the central aperture of the marudai.

     Take this end with the left hand underneath the top of the marudai and bring the other end of the chopstick also under the surface, while gently pulling the silk with the right hand, so that the chopstick is kept in place.

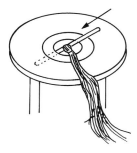 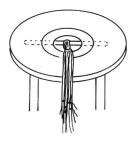

2   **Keeping the silk taut,** separate out the 4 divided groups (two black and two red) and place the bag containing the counterweight on top of the marudai covering three of these groups: this is only a precaution in case the silk is dropped which will result in the displacement of the chopstick, and could lead to problems.

3   Holding the single group, undo the one cotton knot which tied the four divisions of silk together.

4   Gently separate the divided groups of 12 strands of silk from the cotton keeping hold of one group and lay the other ends on the floor keeping them apart (otherwise they will inevitably join and have to be re-counted).

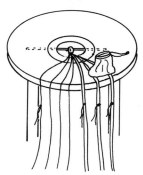

The knot for attaching the silk to the bobbin

1   Take the silk in the right hand and the bobbin in the left hand with about 2cm of cotton extending from between the thumb and the index finger.

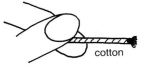

cotton

2   Bring the ends of the silk under the cotton. Hold, with the end of silk being about 5cm.

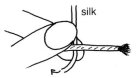

silk

3   Pass the silk tightly around the left thumb, under its own strands and back over the cotton. Hold in place between finger and thumb. The ends of the silk should only extend about 1cm.

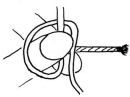

4   Take the cotton end and make a little loop, holding the loop again between finger and thumb with the knotted end just protruding. Slip the silk loop over the top of the cotton loop and slide the knot gently down the silk to tighten it, pulling only the silk. **Do not pull the cotton.**

The result will be a silk knot round a cotton loop. If the ends of the cotton are pulled hard the silk should fall away from the knot. This knot takes some practice not only to learn, but to ensure that only about 1cm of silk is left at the end of the knot. If the ends are longer (which they always are to begin with) they will become caught in the braid towards the end of braiding and besides, silk is expensive and all of it should be used. If like me you find this knot difficult to master do not despair, but attach the silk to the cotton in any way that will tie them together, and practise the knot at a later stage.

Hanging the bobbins from the marudai

After attaching one bobbin the silk should be wound from **underneath** (if the silk has not been wound from underneath the bobbin, this method of hanging the bobbin will not work), and hung from the marudai in the following way:

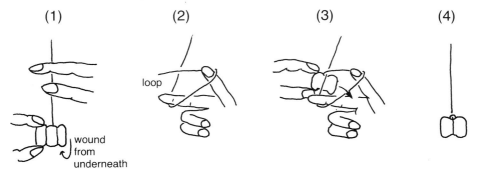

(1) When the silk is about 30cm from the marudai hold the bobbin in the left hand and place two fingers of the right hand on the silk. (2) By making a circular movement, a loop will be formed. (3) Place the bobbin in the centre of the loop – let go – and (4) it will hang of its own accord. If it is too near the top of the marudai it can be lowered by holding the silk and slipping the bobbin down. If it is too far (over 20cm) from the top then undo the loop and try again further up the silk.

Once the bobbin is hanging from the marudai the heavy weight on the other groups of silk can be removed, as the weight of the bobbin will keep the chopstick under the marudai in place. Then attach the bobbins to the 3 remaining groups of 12 strands, either leaving them tidily wound on the floor, or hanging them from the marudai after the knots are made.

Separate out the other divided groups one by one and attach the bobbins, which can then be wound and hung in the same way, adjusting them to make sure that they are all hanging **at the same height** from the marudai. The optimum distance does vary with the braid, but a height of 18cm from the top for *maru-genji* is suggested.

Now the bag containing the weights can be hooked on to the loop, at present containing the chopstick. Take the picture or S-shaped hook and hang the drawstring of the bag on one end, (the smaller end if using a picture hook). Put the other end of the hook through the loop, making sure that the hook goes over all the strands of the loop, and when the weight is hanging securely, remove the chopstick. **Do not remove the chopstick until the weight is in place.**

When this process is completed, the chosen method of braiding should be consulted to see how the groups of silk should be positioned and in which order the colours should be placed according to arrangement (a). It is often difficult to do this neatly, particularly when starting for the first time, and inevitably some strands will be crossed over others.

At last the marudai is set up, and it is time to start braiding by following the stages in the sequence of braiding for your chosen method. The whole procedure of warping and putting on 16 bobbins should with practice take about 20 minutes but you must expect it to take much longer the first time and to involve frequent re-reading of the instructions.

Whenever braidmaking is interrupted for a while the chopstick should always be inserted from the right-hand side under the surface of the muradai, over the point of braiding and under the surface the other side.

 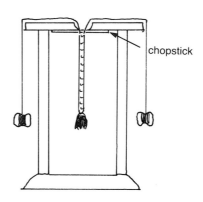

chopstick

Then the weight can be removed. If the weight remains on the braid for any length of time it tends to pull the braid downwards, leaving that part of it with a different tension from those which have gone before and are to come. The chopstick is also inserted to prevent accidents from happening. Without it, once the weight is removed the braid rises to the level of the outside of the marudai and the slightest movement will alter the delicate balance of the bobbins: then braid and bobbins together will fall in a tangled heap on the floor. It is rare to meet a braid-maker who has not had this happen at one time or another.

Possible problems

From time to time through miscalculation or mishandling problems can arise during the procedures described above. Here are some suggestions for coping with specific situations.

1   **Not enough silk has been warped for the number of bobbins required.**

This is easy to resolve. After the silk that has been warped is attached to the bobbins and hung from the marudai, warp the extra amount of silk, winding and dividing it in exactly the same way as before but using a long length of cotton thread when tying all the silk together to make the loop; and take it to the marudai. Slip the loop on to the chopstick which is already in place under the marudai and tie the cotton thread binding the new group of strands to the rest, firmly underneath the marudai. Then bring the silk up through the aperture and wind on to the remaining bobbins.

2   **Too much silk has been warped for the number of bobbins**

Whichever warping method has been used, do not cut off the extra unwanted silk straight away, but pull it back through the marudai and tie it with cotton to the loop in order to keep it away from the initial braiding. If it is very long, wind the silk round one of the pillars of the marudai until a short length of braid has been made. Only then can the extra length be cut off safely and kept for later use.

3   **The silk has been badly divided, and some groups have more or less strands than the number required**

Each group has to be recounted before the bobbins are put on the silk to make sure that an equal number of strands are attached to each; otherwise your braid will be uneven.

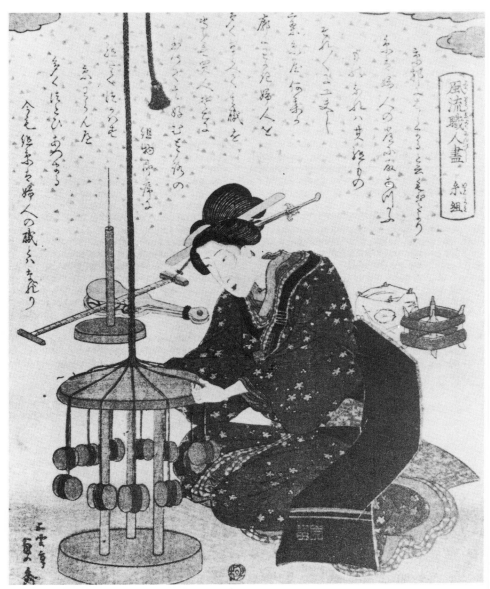

Edo print of a braid maker, using a marudai for upward braiding techniques. In the background kowaku, bodai, weighing and measuring equipment are depicted. Reproduced by kind permission of the Dōmyō School.

TECHNIQUES

A good even braid can be achieved only after practice, and each braid has its own character, not easily revealed without concentration and a desire for perfection. My own first attempts at braid-making were really quite horrible: full of mistakes and irregularity. Nevertheless a genuine fascination with kumihimo combined with perseverance led to a rapid improvement in technique and the results, although by no means perfect, were a basis for ideas and images of how to use the braids in future work.

Sometimes I still despair at my own technique with certain braids, and have to look at my results and analyse the cause of unevenness. Although all braid-makers have to discover for themselves how to improve their work, here are some of my own conclusions on marudai technique, which might help with problems concerning the appearance of a braid.

A glance through the various methods of braiding will reveal that each one has its own layout of groups of threads. If a braid is to be even, these groups **must** be kept in the same geometric relation to one another throughout braiding. As the very nature of braiding on a marudai always entails moving a pair of bobbins from one group and adding them to another, certain readjustments have to be made continually if this relation is to be maintained. If readjustments are not made, the next bobbins to be moved will enter the braid at a different angle from the previous ones and the braid will become irregular in appearance. Readjusting involves lifting all the bobbins belonging to one particular group and replacing them firmly in their original position in the layout of the braid. This also helps to set the stitches that have just been woven. It is advisable to check before starting each new sequence of braiding that all the groups are in the right relationship to each other for that particular braid. The instructions for each method of braiding include indications when readjustment should take place, and these should be followed.

Handling the bobbins

When making any braid on a marudai the silk should be lifted at the point where it joins the bobbin and not where it leaves the surface of the loom, so that the silk and the bobbin are lifted lightly together in your hands and put down in a **controlled** way. While the bobbins are being moved from one position to another the silk should always remain taut, but not stretched or twisted. Pairs of bobbins should be lifted and replaced with the same tension and timing in both hands. The fact that the right hand is generally stronger than the left is often a cause of unevenness in braiding, and at the outset some movements feel considerably more awkward than others, so care should be taken to handle the bobbins in exactly the same way when moving them in any direction.

However complicated a braid is the bobbins will inevitably return to their original positions, and during a sequence of braiding, some pairs of bobbins are moved and others not. Then in the next sequence those that were active previously are not moved while others are; so within every group of bobbins there is an order in which they are incorporated into the braid. If that order is disturbed through the wrong bobbin or pair of bobbins being picked up a mistake will be made which will inevitably show in the finished braid. Sometimes the arrangement of the colours can greatly help in indicating which are the next bobbins to pick up, and these will always be in the lowest position at the point of braiding, however many bobbins are used. Mistakes are so easily made during braiding that the next section of this book is devoted to why they happen and what to do about them.

Lengthening the silk

As the silk is used up in the braid, so the bobbins must be lowered from time to time so that they can be moved during braiding from a comfortable height. This should be done frequently in order to avoid working with lengths of silk which are too short; for it will soon become apparent that the action of moving the bobbins and therefore the tension of the braid will vary according to the length of the silk. Since even a slight alteration in tension will affect the appearance of the braid it is important to take time to adjust the length even though this disturbs the rhythm of braiding. There are two ways of doing it. One is to loosen the loop and move the bobbin gently down the silk, and the other, the approved Japanese method, involves undoing every loop on the bobbin and rewinding further down the silk. The latter method does reduce the possibility of stretching the silk but takes much longer. I well remember the disapproving looks directed at me by my Japanese teachers as I furtively used my short-cut method, but continue to find it satisfactory.

When the bobbins have been lowered, they should again all hang at the same distance from the top of the marudai. It is much easier to pick up a pair of bobbins if they are at the same height, especially when they are out of sight at the back and have to be felt for. It they hang too low the bobbins will swing and twist round each other; if too high the braiding action cannot be carried out easily and the completed braid is lifted with them as they are moved.

Point of braiding

During braiding the centre or point of braiding should hardly move at all. This does depend on the braid, but if any action causes it to lift or shift significantly (except when using 8 bobbins for either *mitake* or *maru-genji* when it is inevitable) too much pressure is being used to move the bobbins and an adjustment of technique is called for. The point of braiding should always be centred after a sequence of braiding has been finished. If it is not, a readjustment should be made, by gently moving the completed braid from underneath the marudai.

Tying on the counterweight

After a while the counterweight will touch the base of the marudai and cease to function as such. This becomes noticeable when the point of braiding rises with each movement instead of continuing to progress downwards and it will feel strange. Although it is obviously important to move the weight up the braid quickly to avoid altering the tension of the braid it is advisable to finish the sequence of braiding first and then insert the chopstick under the marudai but over the point of braiding. The weight can then be removed, the picture or S-hook put away for use on the next new braid, and the counterweight bag tied directly on to the braid with a half-hitch. The large knot which has been made on the end of the drawstring should prevent it slipping off. Try to make sure that the bag hangs evenly from the braid, in the centre.

The weight of the bag will make an indentation in the braid but this can be removed by pulling it while steaming after the braid has been completed.

Untwisting and Twisting the silk

Unless the braiding method specifies otherwise the strands of silk should always lie flat and untwisted on the surface of the marudai. If they become twisted in use – as happens more often with some braiding methods than with others – the silk must be untwisted or the appearance of the braid will be affected in two ways: twisted strands catch the light in a different way and will look different from the rest, and they also form a tighter, narrow group of threads which will make the braid become thinner. To untwist the strands hold the silk on one finger from where it hangs from the top of the marudai and turn the bobbin against the twist until the strands are smooth again. This minimises handling of the silk to be braided which is important if it is not to lose some of its sheen. The same action should be used when twisting the strands according to the directions for certain braids, such as *yotsu, kaku-yattsu* and *maru-yattsu.*

Changing patterns

As discussed, any one method of braiding can yield many different patterns, according to the number and proportion of colours and the number of bobbins used. It is fascinating to see different patterns emerge from one length of silk as colours are moved within the groups to change the arrangement before a new sequence of braiding begins. This can rarely be achieved smoothly in a single braid since bumps in the braid are inevitable as the order of the threads is disturbed when they are being moved to new positions. This is of course of no importance when making samples but will not enhance the appearance of a finished braid unless the changeover can be disguised with a knot or concealed by passing another piece of the same braid over the disturbed part. Some patterns in certain braids can be changed without this problem arising but the possibilities must be worked out beforehand and taken into account when planning a new braid.

It is always wise at a later stage of learning to braid to make a solid colour sample of any method of braiding to examine its shape and consistency before adding other colours, but making a plain braid is far more difficult than one incorporating a pattern, as mistakes are less easy to detect and any unevenness will clearly show in the braid.

Analysing the braid

If a particular braid gives difficulty, or an analysis of its construction is required, marking the bobbins with numbers may be helpful. Use the small round self-adhesive coloured labels available from stationers' and stick them to the lead circles at each end of the bobbin, using different colours if necessary. This will reveal exactly the order in which the bobbins move and where they move to on a marudai before returning to their original positions.

MISTAKES

Whenever a mistake is made, the pattern on the outside of the braid is disturbed, and detracts from the beauty and flow of the braid. There is no alternative when this happens but to undo, find the problem, correct it and resume the braid. Unfortunately mistakes are quite inevitable, especially to begin with, so it is only sensible to expect them and to know how best to deal with them. Usually the mistake is not noticed immediately but only discovered with all the more irritation later, when examining progress. With most patterns, though, it should be obvious that something has gone wrong if the colours do not return to their expected positions (not necessarily the original ones) at the end of a sequence of braiding. 'But what did I do?' is a familiar cry from students.
Here are some likely answers.

1 A step has been omitted from or repeated twice in a sequence of braiding.

2 The wrong bobbin or pair of bobbins has been picked up, thereby disturbing the order of braiding.

3 The wrong bobbin or bobbins have been put down in the wrong place.

4 A sequence has been interrupted for some reason and resumed at the wrong point in the sequence.

5 One group of strands has inadvertently been crossed with another: this can happen during braiding, while adjusting a whole group of bobbins, or through moving the actual marudai.

On discovering a mistake it is best to stop braiding at the end of a sequence and remember that since kumihimo is a logical process braids can be undone as quickly as they are made simply by reversing the sequence. A look at the point of braiding will always indicate which strands were the last to have been moved and which therefore have to be returned first to their former position on the marudai. If the process of reversing a sequence seems to be difficult, draw diagrams and follow those in the same way as when making the braid. Always move the bobbins in pairs, and continue this process (which soon assumes its own rhythm) until the order of undoing is obstructed by other groups of strands. At this point the mistake or beginning of a series of errors has been uncovered. After restoring the groups of strands to their rightful positions undo another sequence or two of braiding to ensure that the mistake really has been located and corrected, for there is nothing more frustrating than to discover later that it was missed and having to go through the whole business again. Fortunately once the problem has been resolved, no trace of it can be seen in the braid afterwards.

Sometimes making a mistake can lead to interesting discoveries: a new pattern or even a new braiding method. If this happens, write down, immediately, the exact movements of the bobbins and the sequence of braiding, or it may be impossible to rediscover the new method. At the very least, undoing a braid does lead to a greater understanding of its construction and this might help to prevent further errors. Here are some preventative measures:

1   Before starting to braid, always tie a length of braid or cotton round one of the pillars of the marudai to indicate which side is nearest you during braiding, in case the marudai is moved.

2   Always finish a sequence of braiding before stopping for any reason of your own.

3   If the telephone or doorbell rings complete the stage of braiding you have reached and quickly write down the number of the next step.

4   Check frequently along the finished part of the braid by moving around and looking underneath the marudai at all sides of the braid to see if any mistakes have been made. If the marudai is to be moved, **slowly** turn it around (otherwise the bobbins will swing and twist) and make sure that the side facing you is returned to its original position.

Natural light is best for braid-making as artificial light changes the colours of the yarn and this can lead to mistakes when working with a group of similar colours. Kumihimo should never be hurried: if it is, mistakes will invariably be made, as though the craft itself were objecting to the lack of respect being shown to it. In Japan, the only sound which accompanies classes is that of the gentle clacking of the bobbins. Kumihimo does demand concentration, and distractions of various kinds with the sole exception of appropriate music do not make for good even braids.

ENDING A BRAID

As the silk comes towards its end and the knots of the cotton bobbin threads appear over the edge of the marudai it is time to measure the finished part of the braid and to allow for the tassel at the end. When the required length of braid has been completed, always finish the sequence of braiding. Then take a length of cotton and make a series of half-hitches round the top of the braid, pulling it down slightly with one hand so as to tie just above the last part woven.

If the pattern of the end of the braid has to match the beginning, always weave a little more before tying off, because the last part of the braid sometimes works loose once the bobbins are detached, with the result that the sewing to secure the end of the braid has to be made at a slightly earlier point.

Before removing the bobbins at the end of a braid, insert the chopstick and take off the weight. If the weight is left on the braid it will pull it slowly downwards as more bobbins are taken off. Pull the cotton ends on the knots to release the silk, in an order that maintains the balance of the bobbins until only two are left. Take hold of these two together and remove the bobbins. If only a very short length of silk is left after finishing the braid, take off the weight without inserting the chopstick, for this will make it difficult to undo the knots, and take care to maintain the balance of the bobbins around the marudai, while taking them off the silk.

After the bobbins have been removed, undo the cotton loop which has been holding them when hanging from the marudai and put them away.

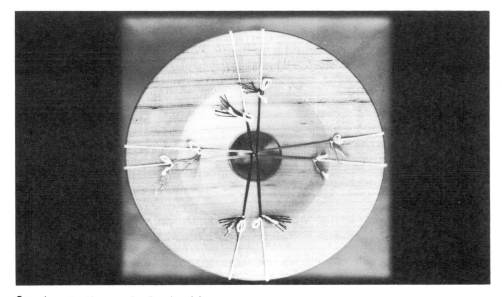

Coming to the end of a braid

Edo print of a seller of braids in a Kyoto shop

FINISHING

The simplest way to finish the ends of a braid is by sewing with a fine needle to secure the woven part and then trimming the ends for a tassel. I thread a needle with the same yarn as one of the colours in the braid and while keeping the white cotton tie on the braid insert a needle through the cut ends, so that after sewing the end of the thread becomes part of the tassel. Then stitches can be made back and forwards through the middle of the braid to secure the woven strands inside, as a hand-made braid will undo itself very quickly if allowed to. A binding of thread can be made on the outside of the braid for a neat tie around it and the needle can then be pushed back and forwards to secure the tie, the end again leaving the braid as part of the tassel. The cotton thread can be removed as soon as the inside of the braid has been sewn enough times to ensure that it cannot undo of its own accord.

Before the ends of the tassels are trimmed the braid can be steamed, which will straighten it and with some yarns can make it more pliable. Steaming will also remove any indentations left on the surface where the counterweight has been tied to it at various points. Paper cut to the required size can then be wrapped tightly and secured round the tassels to enable them to be trimmed so that all the strands will be of identical length.

After steaming I leave the braid for a while to shrink back before attaching it to a garment or object. When attaching braid to another surface, always sew with the finest needles available, invisibly through the braid, making sure that the needle emerges in a part of the braid of the same colour as the thread being used, and that the stitch follows the line of the movement of the silk in the braid. Otherwise the sewing will be visible and detract from the visual effect of the braid. This is a skilled job. If the braid is to be inserted into a seam, ensure that the woven strands are secure inside the braid or it might slowly become loose, even when stitched into a garment. When cutting a braid, **always** sew each side of the planned cut before using scissors, or valuable braid will be lost through fraying.

Once fine kumihimo silk has been woven, especially in a small braid, it is almost impossible to restore it to its original straight condition. Even after steaming it is likely to retain a slight permanent wave, and this must be remembered when calculating and weaving specific lengths.

When the Japanese make obi-shime, they usually add extra silk to the ends of the completed braid to make fuller tassels for a decorative effect. Here is a description of the traditional way.

The braiding is stopped at an earlier point than if ending and finishing a braid as described above, according to the length of your tassel, which must be calculated for each end of the braid when warping the silk.

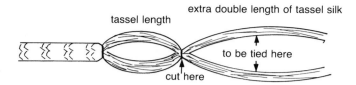

extra double length of tassel silk

tassel length

to be tied here

cut here

The extra two groups of silk to be inserted into the original tassel of the completed braid are bound by the following knots, tied against the tension provided by fixing one end of the yarn to the steel attachment of the bodai (or substitute), in a half hitch.

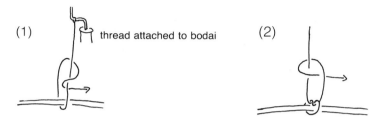

(1) thread attached to bodai

(2)

Then the two groups are tied together (3) and the ends manipulated with a large needle into the shape illustrated in (4). Then the extra silk is ready to be tied to the completed braid.

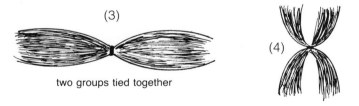

(3)

two groups tied together

(4)

A needle is threaded with 4 strands of silk and again tied round the steel attachment to the bodai and inserted through the centre at the end of the braid. The extra tassel silk is added in the following way by knots (5) and (6).

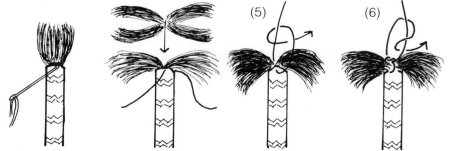

(5)   (6)

Then the full tassels are trimmed, steamed, combed and protected before use by wrapping cellophane around the ends.

NOTES ON KUMIKATA

The Japanese names for braids tend to be either prosaic and practical or highly poetic, relating the shape and movement within a braid to natural phenomena such as streams, clouds and trees. The Chinese characters that are used for the Japanese language are always visually beautiful, possessing a harmony quite their own, but would mean little to the non-Japanese-speaker. The Japanese names are therefore given in romanised form with literal translations, with an indication of the concept behind each name. No English equivalents have been attempted. It might however be worth pointing out that the suffix *gumi* used as part of the formal name of each method in this context means simply 'braid' and is therefore usually omitted in general references.

Explanation of the diagrams used for each braid

For each method of braiding, a set of diagrams is provided showing the sequence of movements which must be repeated in order to make a braid. The circles represent the round surface of the marudai and the dots are symbols for the bobbins. The arrows show the movements for each pair of bobbins, and LH and RH of course stand for the left hand and right hand respectively. The numbers in the circles indicate the progression of the sequence of braiding, and when readjustments have to be made after moving bobbins they are clearly marked.

A series of circles are set underneath the sequence of braiding, and these give a selection of possible arrangements of colours which will produce different patterns, using the same number of bobbins and method of braiding. Examples of the patterns can be seen in the colour photograph of each braid. Two colours are suggested in the arrangements for most braids and these should be moved to the positions indicated before the first stage of a sequence of braiding begins.

Certain arrangements of colours can greatly assist the learning and understanding of the construction of a braid, and also help to prevent mistakes. Bearing this in mind, pattern (a) for all braids has been designed to maximise the help that colours can provide when first making a braid.

Diagrams have also been included for certain braids to show the progression of two colours after one, two or three sequences of braiding. This will enable you to check the correct positions of colours with those on the marudai.

As explained earlier, the most straightforward method of braiding is that for *maru-genji gumi*. As the braiding sequence is simple, especially with the colours positioned as in arrangement (a) and the movements are described in detail it is the most suitable of the 12 braids for those trying a braid for the first time.

Increasing the number of bobbins used for certain kumikata

Some braids can be made with different numbers of bobbins, and when this is possible, the notes on each braid state what combinations can be used. The position of the groups is not altered, but the number of bobbins in each is increased equally, with the exception of kara uchi, where the number of groups is increased. Here is a diagram of *maru-genji,* showing the arrangement when using 8, 16 and 32 bobbins.

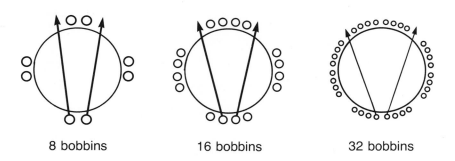

| 8 bobbins | 16 bobbins | 32 bobbins |

The movements of a sequence are not affected: if more bobbins are used it will just take more repeated sequences before the first bobbins return to their original positions. The more bobbins on a marudai the closer together they will be, and greater care must be taken both in readjusting and when lengthening the silk on the bobbins, as it is easy to inadvertently cross over adjacent threads.

Here are similar diagrams for *kara uchi*

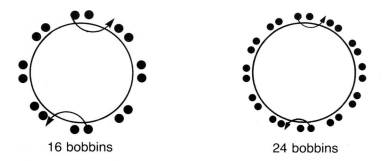

| 16 bobbins | 24 bobbins |

Samples

Samples of the 12 braids were made using a cut length of silk of 100cm for all except *shi-no-nome gumi* (which needs a length of 120cm for 4 bobbins) with 12 strands of silk for each 70gm bobbin. The weights used for making each braid varied, and were chosen to suit its particular construction. As discussed earlier, a recommended weight can only be given as a guide, as individual braid-makers will all have different braiding actions, and this will affect the flexibility of a braid. The weight can also affect the length of stitches on the braid, and the length of the finished braid. To illustrate this point, two samples of *maru-genji gumi* were made with a difference in weight of 220gm: the heavier weight resulted in a braid 6cm longer than that made with the lighter weight. A chart comparing the results of the samples is given at the end of the section on methods of braiding.

Learning a method of braiding

After studying the layout of a new braid, looking at the groups, the number of bobbins in each, the space between them and then positioning the colours on the marudai according to arrangement (a), braiding can begin. As the sequence of braiding is followed, it is a good idea to memorise the movements as quickly as possible, so that the diagrams can be put to one side and concentration can focus on technique, the point of braiding, maintaining the same space between the groups and looking at the movement of the colours within a series of sequences. Memorising which bobbins move to where and at which point in the braid becomes quite easy after a while, and, paradoxically, the more braids that are learnt the quicker this becomes, as they are all related to each other in some way. It is at the beginning that braiding seems to be most complicated. When first attempting a braid it is best to follow the directions slowly and carefully, so as to avoid making mistakes. If after some practice of a particular braid the results do not come up to expectations re-read the section on **Techniques** and also that on **Mistakes** to see if they can help.

The methods of braiding are numbered in ascending order of complexity, although this in itself is debatable, because some braid-makers have much more difficulty with simple kumikata than with those which are more complex. *Yotsu gumi,* using only 4 bobbins, is considered by experienced kumihimo makers in Japan to be the most difficult of all braids to make well, and perhaps should be left for a later stage after practising other braids, although the others too have to be worked on before you will be satisfied with your results.

Suggestions

For first attempts at any of the braids included, try these dimensions:

Cut length of yarn: 100cm
Number of strands per bobbin: 12
Weight of bobbin: 70gm

For *yotsu, kaku yattsu, yattsu rai, kara uchi* and *keiruko no himo* a bobbin hanging height of 15cm is recommended, and for the other braids, around 18cm is a comfortable height. The weight used for each sample is given at the end of the description of all braids, and this should be used as a guide for your own samples. The Japanese have useful words and phrases for describing positions on a marudai, but we have no equivalents in English, so in my descriptions of the stages in the sequence of braiding I have used the points of the compass, **N, S, W** and **E** as being the most universal points of reference.

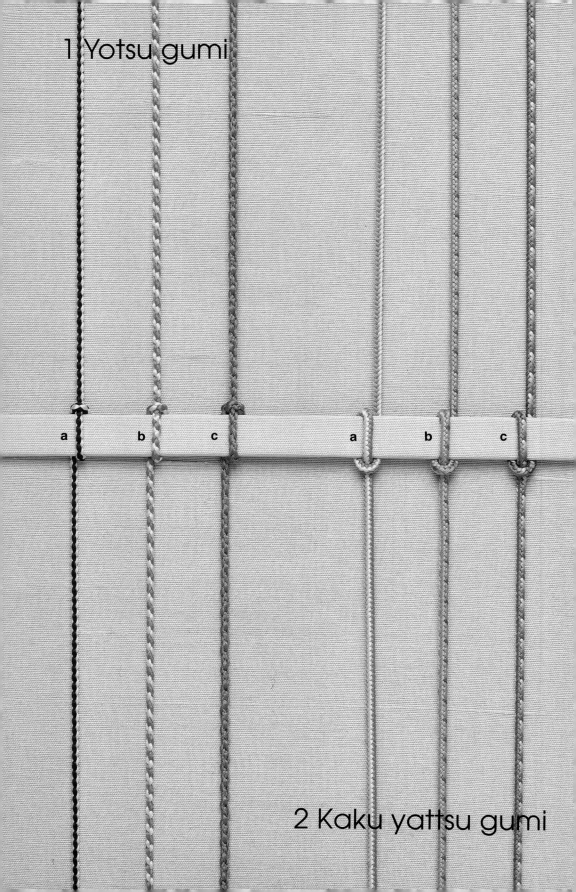

1 Yotsu gumi

a   b   c   a   b   c

2 Kaku yattsu gumi

3 Maru-genji gumi

1 YOTSU GUMI

Yotsu means four, and as this braid is made with four strands it is known simply as *yotsu gumi*. It was one of the earliest braids to be introduced to Japan in the 7th century. Traditionally it was made in one colour and used functionally for tying and wrapping. *Yotsu gumi* is one of the choices of braid suitable for the threading of *inrō*.

Two methods for making *yotsu gumi* are given here: the first has one group of strands at four points on the marudai, and the other uses two opposite positions for the bobbins. Both methods should be learned as only the second can be used in advanced work for splitting the ends of flat braids into effective, tiny individual 4-strand braids.

For both methods of *yotsu gumi* the strands on each bobbin must be twisted before starting to braid, and the arrows on the layout diagrams indicate the direction of the twist. After twisting in the second method the strands should be crossed as shown, with the left strand of the two at the **S** group crossing over the right strand, and at the **N** group, the right strand is crossed over the left. Then braiding can begin. Some strands will inevitably untwist more than others during the construction of the braid, and care should be taken to maintain the same amount of twist for each group of strands throughout braiding. This is particularly important when using many strands of silk to each bobbin.

The sequence of braiding for both methods involves only two stages, and the bobbins should be moved around the surface rather than over the top of the marudai. Do make sure that the finished braid is securely tied with cotton before taking off the bobbins, as *yotsu gumi* will unravel within seconds if allowed, and valuable length will be lost.

With only 4 bobbins, pattern and colour variation is obviously limited. An interesting effect for rather a basic braid can be produced by making a narrow *yotsu gumi* and then using this instead of yarn for one bobbin out of the four needed, and weaving them together as seen in the colour illustration for *yotsu gumi*. A weight of 110gm was used for the sample of *yotsu gumi*.

Point of braiding

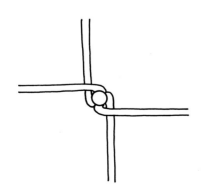

Method 1   Patterns

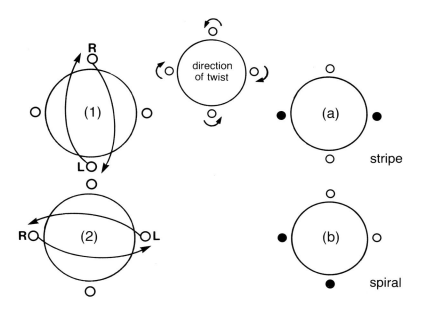

stripe

spiral

Method 2   Patterns

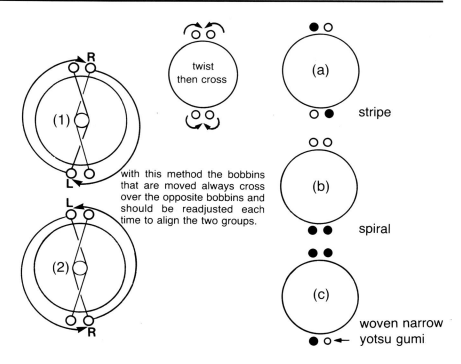

with this method the bobbins that are moved always cross over the opposite bobbins and should be readjusted each time to align the two groups.

stripe

spiral

woven narrow
yotsu gumi

2 KAKU YATTSU GUMI

Square braids must have been very popular in the 8th century, as out of the 360 surviving braids found in the Shōsō-in treasure house, 240 were of a square shape but most were made with a method using more than the 8 bobbins used for *kaku yattsu,* although the general appearance is similar. They look very effective when made with only a few strands of fine silk for each bobbin, using a base colour for 4 or 5 bobbins and contrasting colours for the others, as in pattern (c) where sections of colour move vertically through the braid, on two sides.

As in *yotsu gumi,* the pairs at the north and south sides of the marudai are twisted and then crossed before braiding can begin. The left strand of the S group is placed over the right strand, and in the N group the right strand is placed over the left strand. The two other pairs of strands are not crossed but are twisted. Note the difference between the two directions. The sequence of braiding consists of four stages. The first two entail moving clockwise around the marudai and the last two moving in the opposite direction. In stage (1) the bobbin is just moved to join the next group, and then in (2) the centre bobbin of that group moves right over the next group position so that the crossing of the strands made before starting is maintained throughout the braid. The same actions are repeated, but moving anti-clockwise, in stages (3) and (4). If two colours are used in the arrangement suggested in pattern (a) it will be easier to follow, as one colour will always move in one way and the second colour in the opposite way. Throughout braiding in (a) the colours will always remain in the same positions.

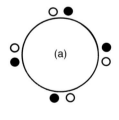

● move clockwise
○ move anti-clockwise

Readjustment of the groups should take place after every stage in order to keep the symmetrical arrangement so as to achieve a good square braid. Although it slows down progress, time must be given to maintaining the twist in each group throughout braiding.

It is interesting to make this braid using pattern (b), as following the path of just one contrasting bobbin will enable you to see more easily how the braid is made. A weight of 225gm was used in making a sample of *kaku yattsu.*

Method

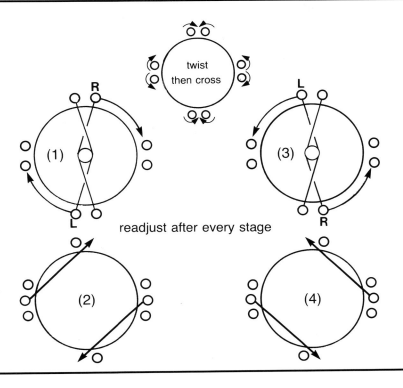

twist
then cross

R

L

(1)

(3)

L

R

readjust after every stage

(2)

(4)

Patterns

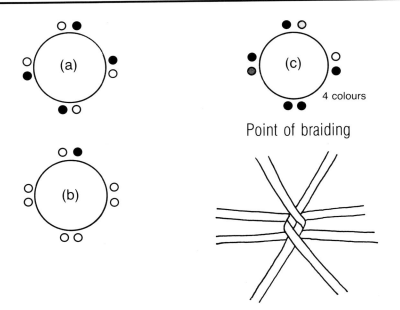

(a)

(c)

4 colours

(b)

Point of braiding

3 MARU-GENJI GUMI

The name 'Genji' has both literary and aristocratic associations for Japanese and was chosen for this strong, 8-ridged round braid when it was devised in the 16th century. One of the easiest to understand and make, it was used on traditional armour with an appropriate *yabane* or arrow pattern. *Maru-genji gumi* is usually made with 8, 16 or 32 bobbins and many different patterns are possible.

The bobbins are always arranged in four groups at the **N, S, W** and **E** points on a marudai, and 4 stages complete a sequence of braiding. The same action is made at each stage: pairs of bobbins are moved from the **inside** of a group to the **outside** of the opposite group. Here is a detailed description of the process.

Stage (1)   Pick up the inner pair of bobbins from the **S** group and lift them right over the marudai to the **N** group, where they are separated and one placed on each side of the group.

Stage (2)   Staying with that **N** group, take the inner pair of bobbins and bring them over to the depleted **S** group, where they too are separated and placed on the outside of the group.

After these two stages it is necessary to readjust the bobbins at the **N** and **S** groups so that the space between the bobbins is the same as in the layout diagram, and the groups are directly opposite one another. Readjustment is made by picking up the whole group with two hands and putting the bobbins down again in a slightly different position. This movement must be made quickly and confidently in all braids, and care should be taken so that neighbouring strands do not cross by mistake.

Stages (3) and (4) move the inner pair of bobbins from the **E** to the outside of the **W** group and then again from the inside of the **W** group to the outside of the **E** group. This movement will feel awkward at first, and you should check if you are using the correct hands for the bobbins as indicated. If two contrasting colours have been used as recommended, and arranged according to pattern (**a**) the movement of colours will look like this:

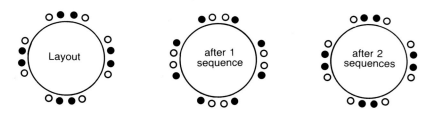

A weight of 550gm was used for the sample of *maru-genji gumi*.

Method

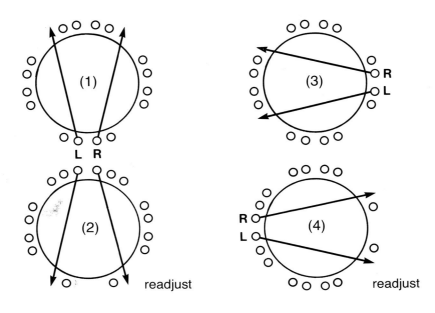

Patterns

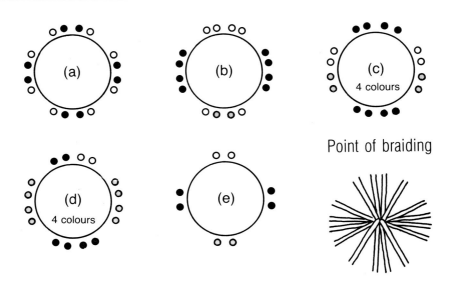

Point of braiding

4 Maru yattsu gumi

c

a   b

5 Yattsu rai gumi

a
b

a

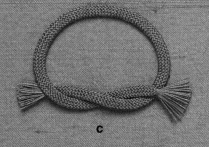

c

d

b

4 MARU YATTSU GUMI

A shiny length of madder-red *maru yattsu* with full tassels provided a stunning effect when tied and knotted around the gleaming black lacquer boxes associated with traditional Japanese life. This round, 8-bobbin braid was used extensively for tying and making decorative knots known as *hana-musubi*. Tightly woven *maru yattsu* provides a stiff yet flexible quality of cord that retains its shape when manipulated into various knots resembling insects or flowers. It is used for the butterfly knot that fastens the little silk brocade bags which protect tea containers used in the Tea Ceremony.

Before a good *maru yattsu* can be achieved, much practice is required, and it is worth persevering with this braid as its method of construction is used as the basis of other braids. As with *yotsu gumi* and *kaku yattsu*, the threads must be twisted in the directions indicated before braiding, and the amount of twist should be maintained throughout construction. *Maru yattsu* is woven in 4 stages: **(1)** and **(2)** moving clockwise, and **(3)** and **(4)** moving anti-clockwise. If two colours are used and arranged according to pattern **(a)** the same colour will always move in the same direction, and the two different colours will always remain in the same places throughout braiding.

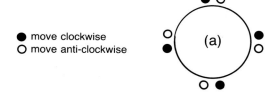

● move clockwise
○ move anti-clockwise

(a)

If the way in which the bobbins are lifted, put down and readjusted is inconsistent, the braid will not have stitches of even length. If you do experience problems, they could be due to stronger movements when using the right hand than with the left, particularly in stages **(1)** and **(2)**. The point of braiding, with its characteristic square shape, should not move from the centre during weaving and should always return to the same shape after every two movements. From looking at the point of braiding it is often possible with *maru yattsu* to see if a mistake has been made. A weight of 260gm was used for the sample of *maru yattsu*.

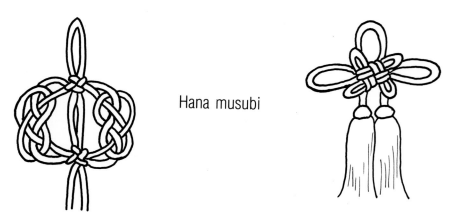

Hana musubi

Method

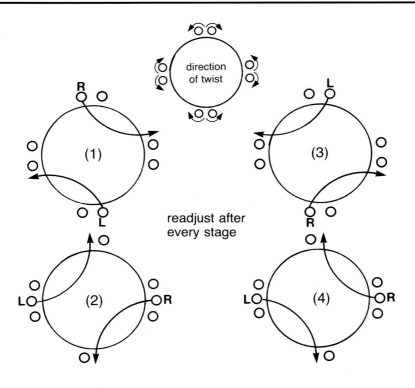

direction of twist

(1)

(3)

readjust after every stage

(2)

(4)

Patterns

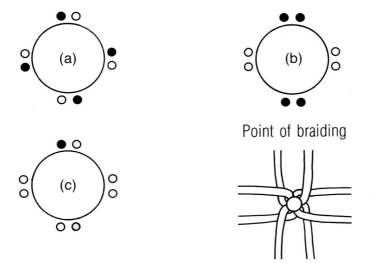

(a)

(b)

(c)

Point of braiding

5 YATTSU RAI GUMI

An image of rushing clear water over pebbles is evoked by the character 'rai' in the name of this braid, and certainly the texture of *yattsu rai gumi* does suggest rounded pebbles. The notion of speed is also appropriate as this braid is quick to make. A limited number of patterns are possible, but when made in one colour there is nothing to detract from the ripples of the surface.

Yattsu rai gumi is a narrow, flat braid, identical on both sides, and it is fascinating to realise that this and the other 8-bobbin braids included in this selection have similarities in terms of groupings, methods and movements around the marudai, and yet the resulting shapes are totally different. However, this likeness can result in problems of remembering and distinguishing one braiding method from another.

Yattsu rai gumi is made in 4 stages. In stage (**1**) the bobbin taken from the **N** and **S** groups moves to the **middle** of the next clockwise group. In stage (2) the bobbin that has just been **passed** is picked up and joins the next group around the marudai. Stages (**3**) and (**4**) consist of identical movements, but in an anti-clockwise direction. After each two stages, the point of braiding will form a slightly diagonal line across the centre, and this should be adjusted so that it is straight by moving the **W** and **E** groups before the next stage, and separating the bobbins slightly so that there is a space in the middle of each pair in which to put down the next bobbin. If using pattern (**a**), here is a diagram which shows the movement of the two colours in the first sequence of braiding. After the second sequence of braiding the colours will return to their original positions.

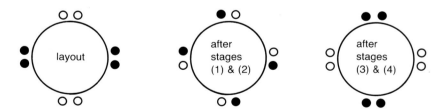

The threads do not have to be twisted before braiding can begin, which is one reason why this braid is quick to make, so an uninterrupted braiding rhythm can be established. A weight of 300gm was used for the sample of *yattsu rai gumi*.

Method

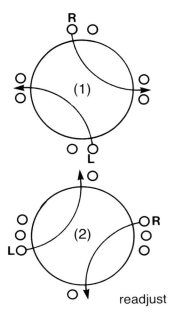

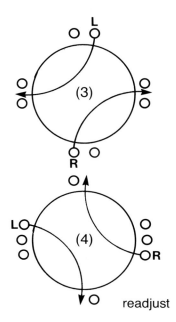

Patterns

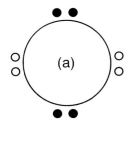

Point of braiding

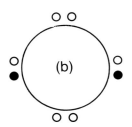

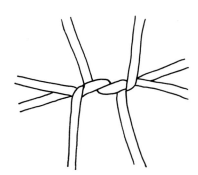

6 KARA UCHI GUMI

The winding zig-zag *yama michi* or mountain road that runs through this braid when certain colours are used is one of the best-known of all Japanese designs, and traditionally conjures up images of historical figures on horseback making dangerous journeys across the mountainous areas in Japan. This is only one of the many possible patterns that can be created with *kara uchi* but is not its principal feature. The word *kara,* meaning empty, refers to the hollow cylinder that is formed while making this braid. It will retain this shape if woven around a core, but otherwise it is finger-pressed flat after finishing. *Kara uchi* can be made with 16, 24 or 32 bobbins.

The layout for *kara uchi* consists of 8 groups of 2 bobbins, arranged symmetrically round the marudai. The sequence of braiding is in two 4-stage parts, and will soon seem familiar to those who have already made *maru yattsu*.

One bobbin is picked up from the **N** and **S** groups and moves over its companion in a clockwise direction to join the next group around the marudai. The three bobbins of this group are readjusted and the centre one is picked up, hops over its neighbour and joins the following group. After 4 of these movements, your hands will be in the starting position to move the other bobbin from the original **N** and **S** groups, repeating the same procedure but in an anti-clockwise direction, completing the sequence of braiding after 4 stages. Here is a diagram showing the progression of colours when arranged as in pattern **(a)**.

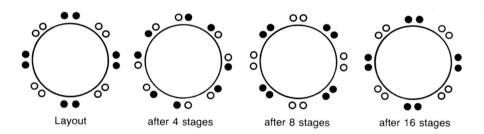

| Layout | after 4 stages | after 8 stages | after 16 stages |

If the colours (when using two as in the above example) do not return to their original positions after 2 sequences of braiding, something has gone wrong. If this happens, look at the point of braiding, which assumes a pretty interlaced circular shape after a few sequences. This will be disturbed if a mistake has been made. After each sequence of braiding, it is advisable to realign the 8 groups, separating them as clearly as possible. As the bobbins in each group should be placed close together a shorter bobbin hanging height is recommended, as if they are too long they will swing and twist around each other. A weight of 450gm was used for the sample of this braid.

Method

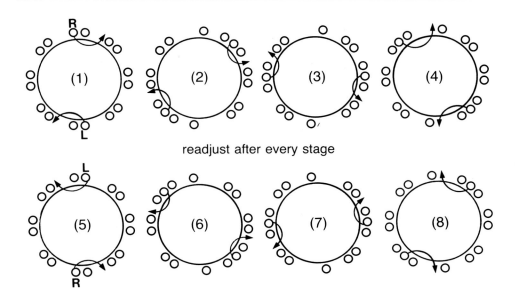

readjust after every stage

Patterns

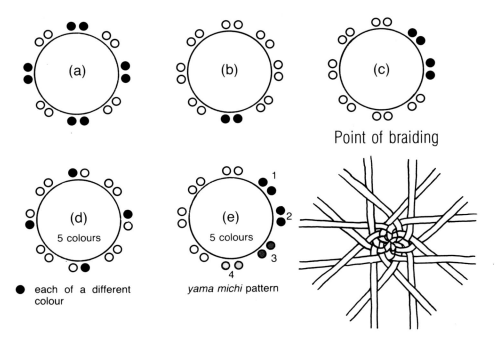

Point of braiding

● each of a different colour

yama michi pattern

7 Keiruko no himo

a

b

c

8 Chidori gumi

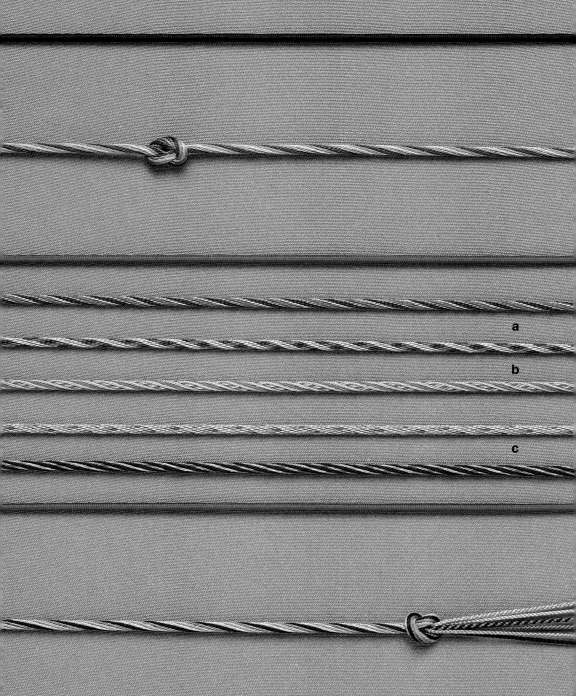

a

b

c

7 KEIRUKO NO HIMO

Dating from the 15th century and also known confusingly as *maru-kara kumi* or *kara uchi,* this strong, tightly knit functional braid is based on *maru yattsu,* but as it is made with 16 bobbins offers more possibilities for patterns and colour combinations.

Concentration is needed when learning this braid, as it is all too easy to slip back into *maru yattsu* by mistake. The sequence of braiding consists of four stages: the inner bobbins are always picked up and move to the outside of the next group; clockwise in stages **(1)** and **(2)** and anti-clockwise in **(3)** and **(4)**. Make sure that the correct bobbins are picked up in stages **(2)** and **(4)**: picking up the wrong ones has caused mistakes in the past in my braids. Two contrasting colours are suggested for a first attempt at this braid, arranged as for pattern **(a)**, so that during each sequence only bobbins of the same colour are moved. The following diagrams show how the colours alternate after each sequence of braiding:

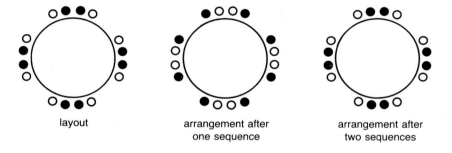

layout   arrangement after one sequence   arrangement after two sequences

If interrupted at all during braiding, check when starting again whether the next stage will be moving in a clockwise or anti-clockwise direction, as if the wrong choice is made a mistake will be made which might not be noticed, especially if working in one colour. Unlike *maru yattsu,* the threads need not be twisted before braiding begins unless twisting is required for a special finish, in which case the bobbins should all be twisted outwards as shown. A weight of 520gm was used for this braid.

direction of twist

Method

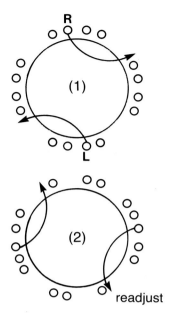

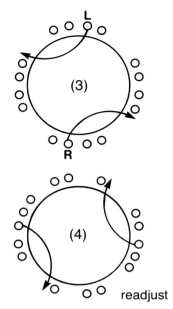

Patterns

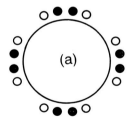

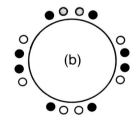

Point of braiding

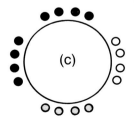

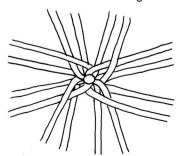

8 CHIDORI GUMI

The 'thousand birds' of *chidori gumi* fly through this purely decorative braid and it is not difficult to see why it was so named. The continual flow and rhythm of its construction also seems appropriate to the concept.

It is not a completely flat braid, but has two flat faces, one slightly narrower than the other, and can be described as having a right and wrong side. It is most effective when used with two strongly contrasting colours, and as it is usually made in this way, the diagrams show the progression of the two colours in order to clarify the sequence of braiding. It is not difficult to memorise or make *chidori gumi,* and then its rhythm can be enjoyed.

The layout consists of four groups of 4 bobbins each at the **N, S, W** and **E** points on the marudai, and each sequence of braiding concentrates on the bobbins in the **N** and **S** groups. In the first four stages of the braid these bobbins are moved in pairs from one side to another, starting with the inner pair nearest you. When this is completed, the bobbins at the **W** and **E** points are repositioned, moving up to surround the **N** and **S** groups as shown in **(5)**. Again starting with the inner bobbins, one each from the **N** and **S** groups, they are moved to make new groups at the sides as in **(6)** to **(9)**. Take care to follow the diagrams accurately for this part of the sequence. Stage **(10)** shows how to reposition the bobbins which have not been used to form new groups at the **N** and **S** points. Then the sequence of braiding begins again with these bobbins.

As you weave, the narrower or wrong side of *chidori gumi* is facing you, so if the marudai is moved round to have a look at progress, it must be moved back again, or the right and wrong sides will change places.

The strands should not be twisted during braiding but be kept lying flat. A slightly heavier weight than usual improves the appearance of the birds, and 600gm was used for the sample.

Point of braiding

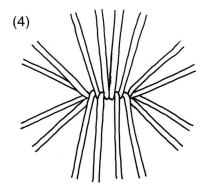

(4)

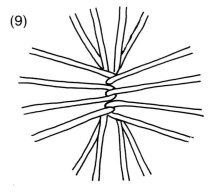

(9)

Method

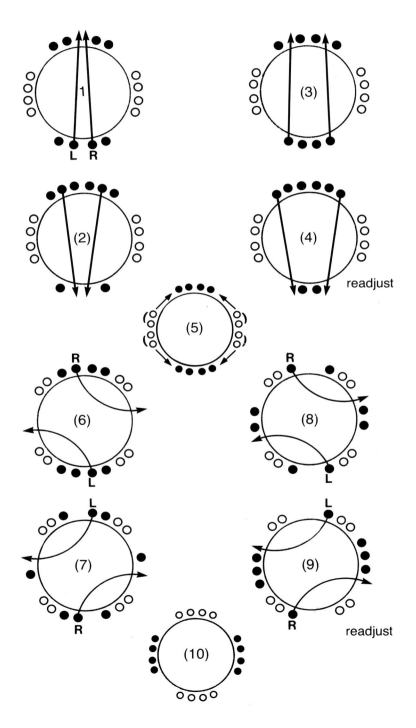

9 KONGO GUMI

The spiral and diamond patterns which can be created with this method of braiding are so attractive and versatile that it has been included in this selection of braids although it does not strictly belong to the group of braids defined as kumihimo according to analysts in Japan. It is a round, dense, extremely strong braid as its name implies (*kongo* meaning ultra-hard); more time-consuming than others, and devouring more yarn in the process. However, the results speak for themselves, and with imaginative use of colour *kongo gumi* can look most effective. Usually 16 or 24 bobbins are used for its construction, but 32 bobbins can also be used.

Eight groups of two bobbins are arranged symmetrically round the marudai, and *kongo gumi* is made from a series of identical actions relating to groups situated opposite each other. At each stage in the sequence of braiding the right hand picks up one bobbin belonging to the furthest group from you on the marudai, and the left hand takes a bobbin from the group directly opposite. The bobbins are moved simultaneously over the surface of the marudai in parallel to join each other's groups. The bobbin to pick up is marked in the diagram, and this should be carefully learnt and memorised in your own way. Do check that your hands move round the marudai in the way shown, **especially at stage (3)** where the right hand moves across the marudai. If using pattern **(a)** the same colours will always be exchanged at every stage of the sequence of braiding.

After a few sequences, look at the point of braiding: if the sequence has been followed correctly, each group will have a set of threads that is in a lower position than the other. This is always the next bobbin to be used in the group. Picking up the wrong bobbin is a common mistake and it will show in the braid as a long stitch compared to those around it. The strands of silk should always lie flat on the surface of the marudai for *kongo gumi;* but they are inclined to twist during braiding and must be untwisted frequently, otherwise the thickness of the braid will vary.

The appearance of the spiral (frequency and evenness of twisting) depends entirely on a really firm readjustment of the groups after each stage. If this is not carried out, the strands on the surface will slowly creep round the marudai and very little spiral will emerge. If a different amount of energy is used for moving from certain positions to others, it will show in the braid as stitches of slightly varying length. Do experiment with colour combinations in this braid: you will be fascinated by the results. A weight of 480gm was used for the sample of *kongo gumi*.

Method

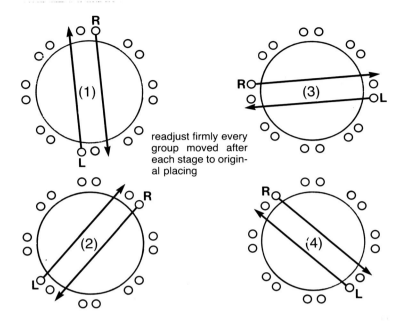

readjust firmly every group moved after each stage to origin-al placing

Patterns

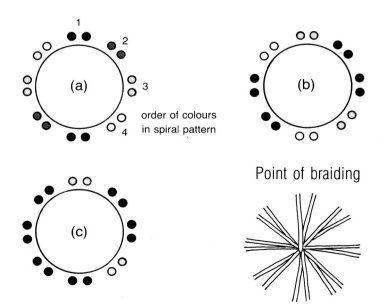

order of colours in spiral pattern

Point of braiding

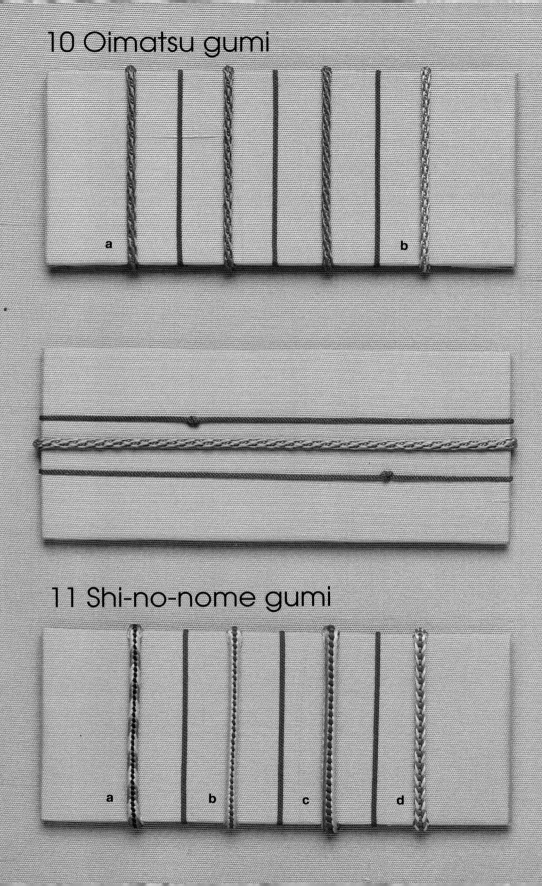

10 Oimatsu gumi

11 Shi-no-nome gumi

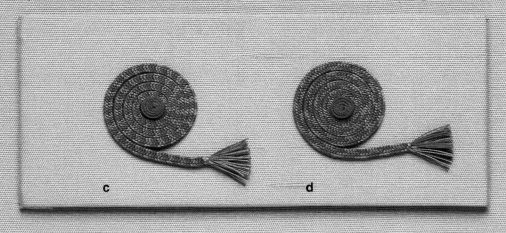

c   d

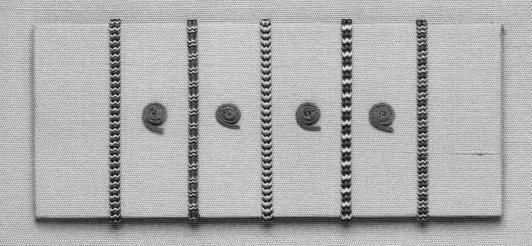

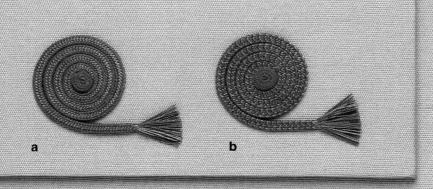

a   b

10 OIMATSU GUMI

The almost gnarled texture which is the main feature of this braid must have led to its being named *oimatsu* or Old Pine. It is both functional and decorative: perhaps at its most beautiful when woven in one colour, but certain patterns are also very attractive.

The principle of the construction of the braid is that an inner core of *maru yattsu* is made by two alternating groups of 8 bobbins. As the 'resting' group is brought up to continue the *maru yattsu* core, its strands form an outer textural spiral effect on the braid. *Oimatsu gumi* is made in two separate parts which are repeated alternately to make the braid. As the use and combining of the groups may seem confusing at first, it is advisable to use two contrasting colours according to pattern **(a)** until the method of braiding is understood. This arrangement will make it easier to see the two different groups used for the construction of the braid, as the same colour bobbins only are used for Part I and the second colour used only for Part II.

Part I: The four two-bobbin groups at the **N, S, W** and **E** points of the marudai are woven as in *maru yattsu* for **three** sequences of braiding, which must be counted as they are made. During this weaving the other groups (NW, SE, SW, NE) are ignored.

Part II: The other four two-bobbin groups which were not used in Part I are now woven also for three sequences of *maru yattsu,* starting with the **NW** and **SE** groups as indicated on the diagram. They will not be tightly knit until the end of the second sequence. The bobbins used in Part I are not used.

The moving from Part I to Part II of this method of braiding soon becomes automatic, as does the counting of the three *maru yattsu* sequences, but if these are not accurate the braid will of course be uneven. Make sure that the 'resting' strands are untwisted as they are brought into action, as any twisting will show on the outside of the braid. When you are confident in making this braid and used to changing from one group to another, then a solid colour braid can be attempted. A weight of 520gm was used for the sample of *oimatsu gumi.*

Point of braiding

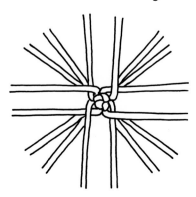

Method

Weave stages 1 – 4 three times   Weave stages 5 – 8 three times

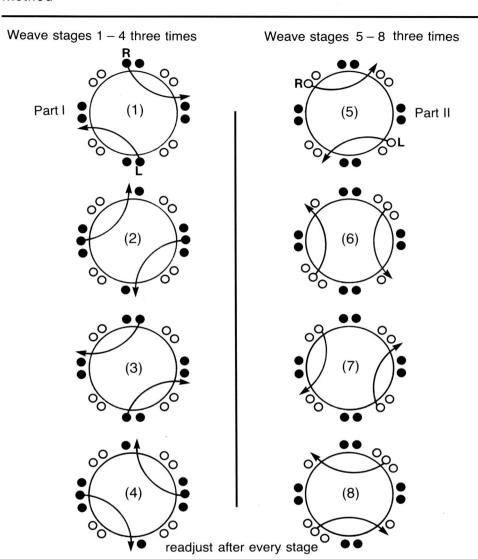

Part I   Part II

readjust after every stage

Patterns

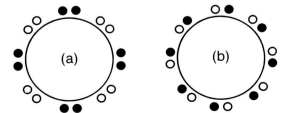

11 SHI-NO-NOME GUMI

The two Chinese characters used in Japanese to write the name of this braid, when read as a compound, mean daybreak or dawn, and *shi-no-nome gumi* is a soft square braid with each of the four sides consisting of a central row of stitches between two ridges. If the same number of strands is used for all the bobbins, the centre row is only just visible, and perhaps this was the image behind the name. Its construction differs from that of other braids in this selection and although it is quite simple to follow and fast to make, skill is needed to weave an even braid, as *shi-no-nome gumi* will clearly show inconsistencies in technique.

The central row of stitches in the braid is made by four bobbins, one each at the **N**, **S**, **E** and **W** points on the marudai, as they swop places in stages **(1)** and **(2)**. Stages **(3)** and **(4)** using the four groups of 3 bobbins need more care, both in picking up the correct bobbins and putting them down in the right places, ensuring that their cross is on the point of braiding, and positioning the hands as indicated on the diagrams. These movements form the outside ridges of the braid, and it is essential to readjust the groups so that they are the same distance from each other and from the four single bobbins. Here is a diagram tracing the movement of colours as used in pattern **(a)**:

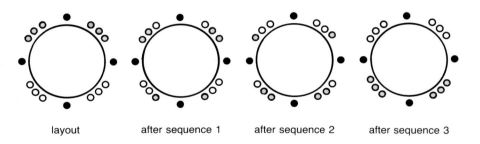

| layout | after sequence 1 | after sequence 2 | after sequence 3 |

A longer length of yarn is needed for the 4 single bobbins. If 100cm is cut for 12 bobbins, then 120cm is needed for the other 4. They can either be wound with the same number of strands as the other bobbins or with more, depending on the effect required. In the colour illustrations of this braid, **(a)** is with the same number and **(c)** is increased by 50%.

Make sure that both stages **(1)** and **(2)** are completed when making this braid: it is quite easy to forget stage **(2)** and this will cause a double length stitch to show in the centre of two sides of the square. A weight of 450gm was used for the sample of *shi-no-nome gumi*.

Method

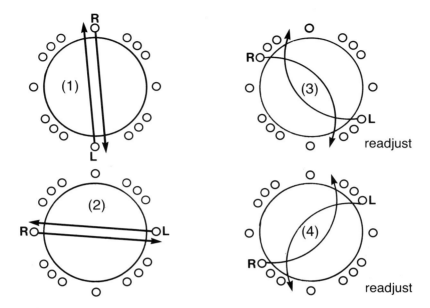

Patterns

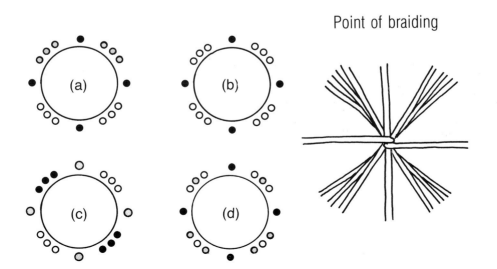

Point of braiding

12 MITAKE GUMI

The first true example of this braid was made in red silk and used as part of a suit of armour dating from the 12th century and presented to the Mitake Shrine, and is therefore known as *Mitake gumi*. It has one of the most rhythmic and satisfying sequences of braiding in kumihimo, but good results can only be expected after practice. There are many variations on this method of braiding, each producing a slightly different appearance in the braid. *Mitake gumi* can be made with 8, 16 and 32 bobbins and many patterns and combinations of colours are possible. With some patterns the two flat faces of the braid are identical, while with others they differ.

The angles between the groups must be maintained accurately if the strands making the side of this braid are to be even. Once the crossing of the bobbins at stages (1) and (4) is mastered, the actual sequence of braiding is quite easy to memorise. However, I and many others found these stages confusing at first, so here is an explanation to accompany the diagrams.

Stage (1) – the cross at the front
1 The RH takes the strands marked (a) and lifts the bobbin up.
2 The LH moves under the RH to take the bobbin marked (b) and then both bobbins are moved over the marudai to their new positions.

Then follow stages (2) and (3) in the diagrams.

Stage (4) – the cross at the back
1 This time the LH moves across to pick up bobbin (c).
2 The RH moves underneath the LH to take bobbin (d). Again the hands uncross in order to put the bobbins in their new positions.

This is more difficult because it is impossible to see what you are doing.

Pattern (a) is not only one of the most attractive that can be made with *mitake gumi,* but also helps to reveal the construction of this braid, as stages (1) and (2) use bobbins of one colour and stages (3) and (4) use bobbins of the other colour. If mistakes are made, take great care in undoing the braid, making quite sure that the stages are reversed in the correct order. A weight of 520gm was used to make the sample of this braid.

Method

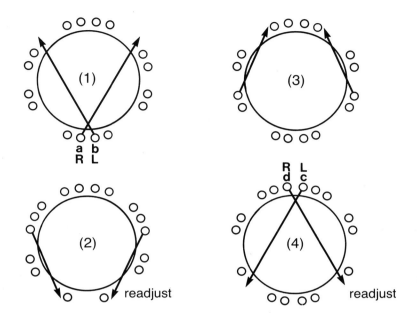

Patterns

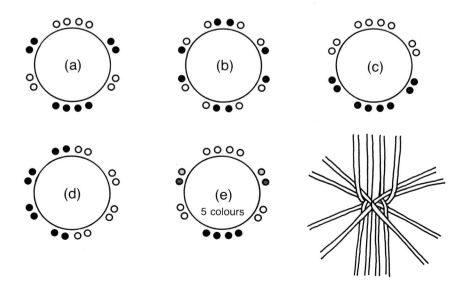

COMPARISON OF SAMPLES OF BRAIDS MADE

	Braid	Bobbins	Strands	Cut length	Result	Weight
1	Yotsu	4 x 70gm	12	100cm	67cm	110gm
2	Kaku yattsu	8 x 70gm	12	100cm	61cm	225gm
3	Maru-genji	16 x 70gm	12	100cm	61cm	555gm
4	Maru-yattsu	8 x 70gm	12	100cm	65cm	260gm
5	Yattsu rai	8 x 70gm	12	100cm	67cm	300gm
6	Kara uchi	16 x 70gm	12	100cm	61cm	450gm
7	Keiruko no himo	16 x 70gm	12	100cm	62cm	520gm
8	Chidori	16 x 70gm	12	100cm	58cm	600gm
9	Kongo	16 x 70gm	12	100cm	53cm	480gm
10	Oimatsu	16 x 70gm	12	100cm	60cm	520gm
11	Shi-no-nome	16 x 70gm	12	100/120cm	67cm	450gm
12	Mitake	16 x 70gm	12	100cm	62cm	520gm

As an experiment, *maru-genji* was made twice, the first time as recorded above using a weight of 555gm. When a weight of 775gm was used the finished length was 67cm compared to the 61cm achieved while using the lighter weight, and the stitches in the braid were noticeably longer.

These are the twelve samples of braid that were made to compile the above chart.

APPLICATIONS

Until now, most of the information contained in this book has been designed to help those who want to know how to make braids, rather than how to use them. While learning the braids, experiments with size, weights, colours and patterns will provide practice and help to build up a sample collection which will be invaluable for future work, and stimulate ideas for possible applications.

Thoughts of putting braids to imaginative use will probably be uppermost in the mind of those contemplating a study of kumihimo, and when it comes to actually making a braid for a specific project, certain considerations must be taken into account and decisions made before the practical process of warping and weaving can begin. Since braids rarely stand alone but are usually attached to other items, thought must be given to the shape, size, texture, strength, colour and patterns which will be required to ensure that the finished braid will add to whatever you are making in the most suitable and appropriate way. I have found when thinking about the choice of braids for a particular project that asking myself the following questions can be helpful.

1   What do I want the braid to do: is it to be functional, decorative, or both?

2   What shape do I want the braid to be?

3   Is the texture important?

4   How is the braid to be attached, and what sort of ending do I need?

5   Do I want a plain or a patterned braid? If a pattern is required, then what sort of pattern do I want, how many colours do I want to use, and in what proportion?

Having thought about these questions, the choice of braid has to be made first, followed by decisions about the number of bobbins to be used, the colour content of the braid, and finally its dimensions. Before making such decisions for yourself, it might be useful to read through the following notes.

Choosing the right braid

The twelve braids described in this book have been selected very carefully from those which can be made with 16 bobbins, so as to provide a balanced introduction to kumihimo. Round, flat and square shapes have all been included, with a view to intriguing the reader, and to demonstrate the versatility of Japanese braids. Choosing the right method of braiding for your first independent project

Buttons, using maru-genji gumi
and mitake gumi on crêpe de chine.

can seem quite a daunting task, but will be based upon the range of samples you will probably have made of all twelve; and of course the more samples in your collection, the easier the choice will be.

If the braid is to be a purely functional part of your project, then unless providing support for the inside of a garment it is likely to be used to hang an item from a certain point, and its strength could well be important. All silk braids are strong, but some are of course more densely woven than others, and the more loosely woven braids do stretch more in use. *Kongo gumi, keiruko no himo* and *maru-genji gumi* are all very strong braids. If a thick braid is required, weaving around a core of less expensive material might be considered as a means of economising on silk; in which case either *kara uchi* or *keiruko no himo* would be most suitable.

It is more likely that you will want your braid to be both functional and decorative, and so considerations of shape, colour, pattern and flexibility will influence your choice of braid. *Yotsu, maru yattsu, kaku yattsu, kara uchi, kongo* and *mitake* should be considered. It is often effective to use more than one method of braiding on a garment but to relate them with colour, or to use the same method but in different patterns or sizes.

Sometimes a purely decorative braid is required, perhaps to be sewn on to a hat or the seams of a jacket. In this case shape, texture and pattern are more important than strength or flexibility. The smaller the item, the less braid will be needed, and so perhaps a more intricate, time-consuming braid using more than 16 bobbins might be used. *Kara uchi* (pressed flat) and *mitake* would be suitable for this purpose, while *Oimatsu, yattsu rai, chidori,* and *shi-no-nome* are also decorative braids.

Choosing the number of bobbins for the braid

The most versatile of the braids described in this book can be woven by using the same method of braiding, but increasing the number of bobbins used. Examples are *maru-genji, kara uchi, kongo* and *mitake,* and they have been given more colour illustration space in order to show the possibilities available for patterns.

When different numbers of bobbins are used with the same braid, they have a dramatic effect on the resulting texture as well as increasing the number of possible patterns. When *maru-genji gumi* is made with 8 bobbins a delightful loosely-woven heart-shaped pattern can be obtained, while with 16 bobbins more designs are available and the texture of the braid is heavier. With 32 bobbins a stiff and solid braid results even when using a heavy weight, and of course the patterns which can be made with 32 bobbins are even more numerous. Other braids show comparable variations when made with different numbers of bobbins, while size is also related to the number of bobbins used, particularly if only one weight of bobbin is available.

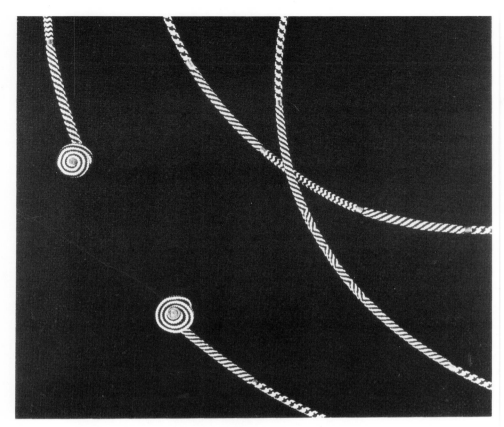

Close up of part of a series of neck circlets using 16 bobbin braids.

Choosing colours

This is obviously a highly subjective matter, relating directly to the way in which the braid accompanies other textiles or items. However, some do find choosing colours difficult when starting to learn kumihimo, so here are a few thoughts on the subject.

Using more than two colours in a braid is both a delight and a headache. So often colours which seem to blend beautifully when brought together in skeins or reels do not produce so harmonious an effect when woven; or similar colours which look as if they ought to produce a deliciously subtle effect in combination end up looking insipid in a braid. One way of avoiding unfortunate choices is to take small lengths of various colours, twist them individually to simulate groups of strands and then together to see the effect. With experience and after many experiments one does develop a sense of which colours will work together well in certain methods and patterns, but there is always an element of unpredictability, and the excitement of actually seeing those first few woven centimetres never diminishes.

Apart from the acquisition of a good technique, the sense and use of colour is probably the most difficult element in braiding. It is important to realise that the smaller the braid, the stronger the colours must be if they are not to be lost in the final effect; whereas softer colours combine better together when more of each can be seen. It is interesting to experiment by making a 32-bobbin braid, using four colours each on eight bobbins, and move the arrangement of colours around every few centimetres not only to see the different patterns emerge but also to compare them and see how the different colours predominate in turn and seem to change as they become adjacent to others. For an example of this, turn to the colour illustrations of *mitake gumi* and compare the ten different samples made from the same warp. It is only after experiments such as these that the full potential of using colour in a braid can be realised, and used for the exact effect required in your work.

Calculating the length of silk to be cut

After deciding on the length of braid needed for your project, the length of yarn to be cut must be carefully calculated from your own records of samples you have made. The chart comparing the results I achieved when producing samples of each method of braiding should be used only as a guide. Your own results will undoubtedly differ, reflecting your own individual style of braiding. However, it can be seen from the chart that if using 16 bobbins, 100cm of warped yarn will produce on average about 60cm of finished braid if all the bobbins use up the silk at the same rate. Exceptions to this are *shi-no-nome gumi* which needs extra silk for certain bobbins, and *kongo gumi* which consumes more silk than other braids. Varying the counterweight can make a considerable difference to the length of the finished braid, as my experiments with *maru-genji gumi* demonstrate, and this should be taken into account when calculations are made.

Because it is so difficult to be exact, I have found from my own experience that adding an extra 10-20cm to the cut length is a sensible precaution against finding oneself in the infuriating situation where, nearing the end of a braid, it suddenly becomes obvious that through a miscalculation the silk is going to run out before the required length has been made. When this happens, there is nothing to be done if the braid is to appear as one piece in your project but cut a new, longer length and start braiding again. Cutting extra is not the extravagance it might seem: after tying off the completed braid and tassel length the extra can be used to make a sample of another braid with the same number of bobbins, or to try another pattern. Doing this indeed often provides some relaxation after the concentration needed to produce a perfect length of braid.

Screen of a kumihimo workshop reproduced by kind permission of the
Suntory Art Museum, Tokyo.

CONCLUSIONS

If by the time you read this section you have attempted even some of the braids described, you will already have discovered for yourself some of the fun and frustration of making braids the Japanese way. Moreover, even if your own results are not quite as you would wish, new ideas, images, colour combinations and possible practical applications will have flashed through your mind at some point, accompanied by the exciting speculation 'I wonder what would happen if . . .?' which for me has often been the prelude to a really interesting development. This is still constantly happening when I'm working, and I feel that even after some years of braiding every day I've only just begun to realise the possibilities of kumihimo.

As with so many other disciplines, a feel for braiding cannot be taught. It is either there or it isn't. Much has been written about the various concepts behind the Japanese arts and the mysteries, philosophies and rituals surrounding them, and there is a wealth of material available in English to anyone interested in the subject. I have myself obviously been deeply influenced by living for four years in Japan, and sometimes find it difficult to convey to others the sense of harmony and perfection which is so natural there and shows itself in so many aspects of Japanese life. Just as the greengrocer discards any of his stock which is blemished or misshapen in any way, so the fishmonger takes pride in providing the customer not only with the freshest but also the most beautifully filleted fish, pulling out the bones with special tweezers; and it is the same deep-rooted cultural impulse which motivates the braid-maker working quietly away to produce a good piece of braid which will serve its purpose admirably.

When people are seeing kumihimo demonstrated for the first time I am often asked 'How can it possibly be commercial? It takes so long!' Again, in Japan such a question would not be asked. The pursuit of a discipline for its own sake is an end in itself, and in artistic matters too the activity is just as valuable as the product. Unless one has seen a great many hand-made braids – which is not so easy in the west – it is difficult to imagine the startling difference between an ordinary piece of work and one which is not only woven without mistakes but through which the spirit of the braid-maker simply shines. While I was studying in Japan, Mrs Dōmyō once showed me one of her 'treasures'. This was a flat, extraordinarily complex braid made in double *kara kumi* on a large marudai by a 78-year old lady. She has since died, but that remarkable piece of himo will continue to be shown to students to inspire them to aim at the highest standards of quality and insight in their own work. Recently in the British Museum I was shown another piece of braid. It is not on public view, but hidden away in the labyrinth behind the glamorous display panels and cases, and it too offers a moving glimpse into the state of mind of its maker. This braid is flat, was made on a takadai, and the method of braiding used is known as *kikko gumi*. This produces a thick, tough, double-sided braid which was often used to attach a sword to a samurai's armour and was popular in the Edo period (1600-1868). The word *kikko* means 'turtle', and the turtle in Japan symbolises long life and is therefore an auspicious emblem for military men. In addition, though, the braid I saw subtly incorporated indications of another pattern into the weaving: that of a *yama michi* or mountain road. It was quite obvious that the samurai for whom it was made was off on a dangerous expedition across mountainous country and that the braid-maker had this in mind when planning and weaving it.

A few months ago in London I was privileged to examine the large private collection of a leading expert on samurai armour, and was fascinated while scrutinising the same method of braiding used for various parts common to all sets of armour to note the differences in the quality of the work and the way in which each maker's individuality showed through. It is experiences like these which can transform a long grey day of repetitive braiding into one filled with reflections and curiosity about the braid-makers of old Japan and their status in towns, villages and the social hierarchy: how indispensable they must have been, and what the whole process of silk production, dyeing, winding and weaving must have been like. Were there rush orders when preparations were under way for a battle? Were some colours available only in certain parts of Japan depending on the local climate and plant life, or were dried plants ordered from other towns and villages with the resulting anxiety about delivery dates? Were kumihimo makers so specialised that if different methods or designs were wanted it was necessary to approach more than one master? If the local warlord was to receive high-powered emissaries from the Shōgun and needed a new outfit to wear or suit of armour to offer as a present, was one of his staff sent off to the leading master of kumihimo who received him with appropriate tranquil courtesy and the moment he left rushed off in a tizzy to check on supplies? So little is known about these aspects of kumihimo that speculation is an endless source of dreams.

When all is said and done, though, it remains a real privilege to learn the techniques of braiding devised by experts so long ago and to use equipment which has changed so little in appearance over the centuries; and to realise that braid-makers are still maintaining the tradition although in such different circumstances of mass communication and the mind-boggling technological advances which change our lives each year. Looms are still hand made from wood and bamboo and not mass-produced in plastic, and silk has been produced for thousands of years, enabling braid-makers to enjoy the sense of continuity which is surely essential for a peaceful existence. When weaving in exactly the same way as the braid-makers of the past I am always conscious of experiencing the same kind of thoughts and visions which must have coloured their lives, and above all the continual search for quality and perfection inspired by the knowledge that the greater the weaver's humility and respect for kumihimo, the more will be revealed.

Catherine Martin was born in London, England. After a difficult decision between a career in music or art, she chose music and went to study at the Guildhall School of Music. She was awarded a postgraduate scholarship by the Hungarian government to continue her studies in singing at the Franz Liszt Academy of Music in Budapest. After 18 months she returned and began working in music-theatre, musicals and opera.

After six years of working in the theatre, she went to live in Japan and appeared in musicals, television and films there. The visual harmony of so many aspects of traditional life began to affect her ideas, and through a series of coincidences she started braiding and didn't stop. After 4 years in Japan she returned to England in 1983. Her first aim was to introduce *kumihimo* to a wider public through exhibitions, teaching and writing. She also began to experiment with dyeing and braiding, extending and developing techniques learnt in Japan to produce unique ways of making and using silk braids. Her braided pieces and circles have been widely exhibited in England and the USA and are in many private and public collections including that of Jack Larsen in America, the Crafts Council in England and the Victoria and Albert Museum. Catherine Martin has recently been collaborating on pieces with Lucy Goffin (textile artist) and Charlotte de Syllas (jeweller). Restoration of Japanese armour for museums and antique jewellery form other aspects of her work which is usually specially commissioned. She still dyes all the silk she uses with natural dyes.

In 1986 she was awarded a grant from the Great Britain Sasakawa Foundation which enabled her to return to Japan for further research into the historical aspects of *kumihimo*. Her contemporary work has been selected for the Crafts Council Index of designer-makers and can be seen on slides at their headquarters in London. In 1991 she was awarded first prize in the UK Platinum Award.